YOUR COLLEGE JOURNEY

A Guide to Surviving
and
Thriving at Berry College

Fourth Edition

Edited by Katherine Powell

KENDALL/HUNT PUBLISHING COMPANY
4050 Westmark Drive   Dubuque, Iowa 52002

CONTENTS

PREFACE

Your College Journey

Katherine Powell
Director, Office of First-Year Experience

In February 1803, Congress approved President Thomas Jefferson's request to fund an expedition to explore the territory west of the Mississippi River. He named the expeditionary group "The Corps of Discovery" and appointed Meriwether Lewis its leader. From the comfort of the 21st Century, it's hard to grasp just how daunting the task of the Corps was. There was no reliable map of the territory, and there were reports that everything from wooly mammoths to the lost tribe of Israel could be encountered there. Because no one was sure how big the continent was it was difficult to predict how long it would take the Corps to fulfill its mission of reaching the Pacific Ocean. Two hundred years before you began packing your belongings to come to Berry College, Lewis and his co-captain William Clark were working to assemble the materials, personnel and knowledge that they hoped would carry them safely into the unknown and back.

Like the twenty-nine men and two women who crossed the continent with Lewis and Clark more than 200 years ago, as a new college student you are embarking on an expedition into unfamiliar territory. Like the Corps of Discovery, you will surely face obstacles you didn't foresee; you may find that you miss friends, family and your old way of life much more than you imagined or that your previous schooling did not prepare you for the academic demands of college the way you thought it would. At the same time, you will certainly discover rewards you hadn't envisioned. You may uncover talents and interests you didn't know you had; ideas you encounter here may lend new insight into longstanding concerns or problems, and you will surely make new friends, form new relationships, and find old relationships strengthened in unexpected ways.

Consider this text and the first-year seminar course in which you are enrolled as tools designed to help you navigate this new terrain. Many parts of this book are intended to serve as a map for your college journey. You'll find essays by Berry students, faculty, staff, and administrators that not only help you to locate the campus services and opportunities available, but also to negotiate the academic, social and personal challenges that lie ahead on the road to graduation. Likewise, discussions with your first-year seminar classmates, instructor and mentor will prove helpful as you plot your course.

Both first-year seminar and this text can serve as a sort of compass, another crucial navigation tool. A compass works by locating a fixed mark (the earth's magnetic pole) by which travelers can orient themselves and gain a general sense of direction. To give direction to your college journey, you will likewise need to find some fixed point to guide you. The purpose that you attach to your education will be that fixed mark, and that purpose in turn is informed by the values you hold and the beliefs and principles that are important to you. Neither first-year seminar nor *Your College Journey* can give your education a purpose, but the readings, exercises and opportunities for discussion and reflection can help you determine your own purpose and direction.

By now it should be clear to you that the notion of the first college year as a journey of exploration and discovery is the guiding metaphor for this text. You'll find references to the journey throughout the book. Enjoy the trip!

A Note about This Text

Most of the selections in this book were written by Berry students, faculty, administrators and staff. Each essayist's role at Berry will be noted at the beginning of his or her piece. These pieces provide an inside view of college life in general and Berry in particular. Also included are some articles and essays by writers outside of the Berry community. These selections will be prefaced by a brief introduction to the author, when appropriate.

No two people experience college in quite the same way. Throughout this book you will find short personal reflections by faculty, staff, and students about their own college experiences. I hope that these pieces, entitled "My College Journey," will help you to see Berry as a diverse community of unique individuals, forging their own paths toward success.

This book also contains a number of worksheets and exercises that invite you to reflect on, respond to or extend the ideas in the readings. To get the most out of this book and your first-year seminar course, make use of these opportunities. What you get from this book, this course, indeed the next four years, depends a great deal on what you give.

Katherine Powell
Director, Office of First-Year Experience

MY COLLEGE JOURNEY

Clarice Ford, Director of Multicultural Student Affairs

When I arrived at college, I was afraid to ask for help, to say no to the party people and yes to the study circles. I failed every class including tennis! The hole I had dug for myself was difficult to climb out of and I quit school. Every door of advancement in the job sector was closed in my face because I did not have a college degree. As I returned to college later on in life, a professor placed a small yellow stickem in my hand with the letters WIT written in black ink. She said "Whatever it takes for you to graduate . . . long nights, early rises with the sun, you must graduate in order to win this race." Those three letters were motivation to win the race not just once but four times (associate, bachelor, masters, doctorate).

Academic Goals for First Semester

Name: _____ Date: _____

Target GPA at the end of this semester _____.

Courses enrolled in this semester:

Course	Anticipated Grade	Credits	Grade points (credits × grade value*)
TOTALS			
GPA (Total grade points divided by total credits)			

*Grade Value: **A** 4.0, **A−** 3.7, **B+** 3.3, **B** 3, **B−** 2.7, **C+** 2.3, **C** 5, **C−** 1.7, **D+** 1.3, **D** 1, **F** 0

Which course do you expect to be the easiest for you? Why?

Which course do you expect to be the most difficult? Why?

List three things you can do in your most difficult course to try to earn your target grade.

1.

2.

3.

List three behaviors you can adopt this semester to bring you closer to your desired GPA.

1.

2.

3.

Quick Tip

Get To Know Your Professors

Set a goal each semester to get to know at least one of your professors well. Forming personal connections with faculty will help you to stay engaged in class, give you important contacts on campus and just generally enrich your college experience. And those connections may come in handy four years from now, when you need references for graduate school or for your first job. *For more on getting along with professors, see Chapter 8.*

UNIT 1

CHARTING A COURSE

INTRODUCTION

It was a favorite saying of one of President Jefferson's twentieth-century successors, Dwight Eisenhower, that in war, before the battle is joined, plans are everything, but once the shooting begins, plans are worthless. The same aphorism can be said about exploration. In battle, what cannot be predicted is the enemy's reaction; in exploration, what cannot be predicted is what is around the next bend in the river or on the other side of the hill. The planning process, therefore, is as much guesswork as it is intelligent forecasting of the physical needs of the expedition. It tends to be frustrating, because the planner carries with him a nagging sense that he is making some simple mistakes that could be easily corrected in the planning stage, but may cause a dead loss when the mistake is discovered midway through the voyage.
—Stephen Ambrose
Undaunted Courage: Meriwether Lewis, Thomas Jefferson, and the Opening of the American West

Some students arrive at college with very clear plans: they know what their major will be, which professors they want to take, and what kind of career they intend to pursue after college. Some have even plotted out a sequence of courses and other requirements they'll need to meet to graduate on or ahead of time. Other students have far less definite plans. They want to earn a degree, but they haven't yet chosen a major. They may not even know which general education courses they need to take or what electives are open to them. Whether you fall into one or the other category or somewhere in between, there are two points in Stephen Ambrose's observation above that you would do well to keep in mind:

Planning Is Essential

Whether you're heading into battle, trekking across a continent, or beginning your college education, careful and deliberate planning now can prevent any number of frustrations later on. We've all heard stories of students who didn't graduate on time because they were just one or two credits short of graduation requirements or hadn't accrued the requisite number of cultural events credits. Others were unable to take advantage of a great internship or study-abroad opportunity because they didn't have the necessary prerequisites. A little foresight can prevent such problems.

Plans Are Subject to Change

If you arrived at SOAR this summer with a whole list of courses in which you planned to enroll, only to find that they were all closed to you, you've already discovered this truth: no matter how carefully you've mapped out the next semester, year, or four years, there are sure to be some surprises. The new ideas and new people you encounter here at college may cause you to rethink your future. New opportunities may open to you that require a major shift of plans. And yes, some things, like course availability are out of your control. Good plans have to be flexible, capable of being adapted to new circumstances.

The readings in this unit focus on two necessary steps in the planning process: knowing what you're trying to accomplish and setting realistic and timely goals for reaching that end. The selections in *Reading One* ask you to think about the purpose of a higher education and to reflect on your reasons for coming to college. You'll be asked to consider Berry's mission statements and you'll have an opportunity to reflect on your own mission as a college student. The second set of readings asks you to consider specific goals that mission entails and introduces some strategies for managing your time to achieve those goals.

QUICK TIP

Get A Tutor

The Academic Support Center provides free tutoring services for all Berry students. Tutors may be students who have had the particular course and done well, majors in the discipline, and/or students who may have a particular expertise in the field (i.e. native speakers of a language). While you are responsible for your own education, a tutor can provide advice to improve your reading and note-taking skills and help you solve problems or understand concepts that are difficult for you. Language tutors can help you with conversation and grammar skills. Tutoring is most effective when you meet regularly, generally once a week, and if you come prepared with specific questions and a copy of the work you need help with. Find a tutor who will work with you once a week. *To find a tutor, stop by the Academic Support Center in Krannert 326 or call extension 4080 or email tutoring@berry.edu.*

THE VALUE AND PURPOSE OF AN EDUCATION

An Uncommon Path

Stephen Briggs

President, Berry College

As a student at Berry, you have joined a distinctive community that extends back more than a hundred years. You are now part of Berry's story, and Berry will increasingly become part of your story. As you read this essay, I want you to consider how you will use your time here at Berry.

During your high school years, you pursued a variety of goals and experiences that define, in part, who you are now as a person. In recent weeks, you have likely introduced yourself to others in terms of where you are from, what you are good at, what you enjoy, and what you have accomplished. As you begin college, you have an opportunity to consider anew what you will become over the next four years. You are in a much better position to choose a path through college than you were to choose a path through high school. You are more mature in your thinking and self-understanding, and you have a broader variety of options to explore. When you graduate four years from now, how do you want to describe yourself? Of course you will have completed a major since that is a college requirement, but what special experiences and goals and accomplishments will set you apart? What will you be excited to include on your resume or in a letter of application to an employer or a graduate school? What will be distinctive about your time here at Berry that will shape you as a person and stretch your imagination and capabilities?

Objectives Berry Freshmen Considered to be Essential or Very Important

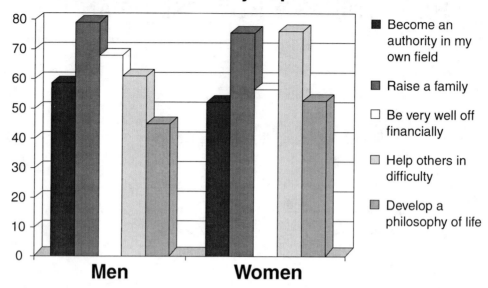

A century ago, the path through Berry was not easy. Students came to Berry because they were thirsty for an education that would open the door to a wider world of opportunities. It was an uncommon path. Students traded two days of serious work on campus for four days of serious education. Berry students built a number of Berry's buildings and cultivated the campus we enjoy today. They cleared the land, made the bricks, grew the food, cooked and cleaned, and maintained the infrastructure. Their work on campus became part of their education and their success. Over the years, the students also achieved considerable success after Berry. Some went on to establish successful businesses based on the practical work skills they acquired at Berry while others became doctors, judges, and teachers. A remarkable number went on to earn doctoral degrees in areas such as physics and animal science. That is why generations of alumni are so passionate about Berry. I have heard individuals time and again recount with great emotion how their years at Berry marked a turning point in life.

Martha Berry's aspiration was to instill in young people a sense of confidence coupled with personal and social responsibility. Her educational philosophy—an integrated education of the head, heart, and hands—was crafted with that aspiration in mind. She was ahead of her time in that she anticipated the value of combining learning experiences inside and outside of the classroom. She grasped intuitively that intellectual skills and practical skills could be combined to powerful effect. Berry's educational plan has always emphasized the importance of its students becoming productive and engaged citizens, the sorts of people who form the backbone of a community and are known for their work ethic, moral character, integrity, ingenuity, generosity, and willingness to serve.

The academic program here at Berry is based on the highest form of learning for undergraduate students—the study of the liberal arts and sciences. Do not be misled by the term *liberal*. In this context it has nothing to do with one's political leanings. Liberal education originally referred to the study of academic disciplines—such as philosophy, history, and mathematics—reserved for free persons of relatively high social rank. Over time, liberal education has come to focus on the core disciplines that examine the natural and social systems of our world. Although we live daily within these systems, we often take for granted and as natural the language and culture of our home as well as the economic, political, and social institutions that have defined our experience.

At Berry, we ask you to complete courses in a variety of disciplines (general education) to expand your understanding of these subject areas and methods. This approach enables you to think critically about your own assumptions in particular areas. We also want you to complete at least one major to give you depth. Whether you concentrate on the liberal arts and sciences (humanities, arts, social sciences, natural or mathematical sciences) or a professional area (such as business or education), study in the major teaches you the tools of a discipline so that you can analyze problems rigorously, understand concepts in their complexity, and communicate ideas precisely.

As part of your academic experience, I urge you to seek out *immersion* experiences. One of the most powerful of these is studying abroad in which you live for a semester in an unfamiliar place with a family whose language and customs are foreign to you. The experience will likely be disorienting at first as unexamined assumptions are exposed. Studying abroad helps you to see your home, your nation, and yourself from a distance, providing a new perspective. Last year, a group of Berry students met in a local jail in a combined class with student-inmates to study inequality, crime, incarceration, gender, and race. This class, too, was a powerful immersion experience. Other students immerse themselves in significant service projects that transform both our local community and the students who participate. Still others spend a year with a professor-mentor immersing themselves in a research project in order to understand research and learning at a whole new level of depth.

In addition to shaping for yourself a rich academic experience here at Berry, I also encourage you to work while at Berry. Work complements your academic program by providing practical problem-solving skills and fostering the development of personal traits that are important—dependability, attention to detail, teamwork, decision making, and initiative. At graduation, many students have found that their work experiences set them apart when applying for jobs or graduate school. While it may be easy to understand how a student in animal science or accounting will benefit from work related to their subject, a student in history or philosophy may not see an obvious connection with their campus job. However, gaining work experience, with increasing levels of responsibility such as project management and supervision, will prove valuable regardless of your major. For students in the humanities, work experience may be the means by which you translate the strength of your liberal arts education into a career path at graduation. The variety of work opportunities on campus will also provide a simple means by which to explore career options with minimal risk.

Warren Buffett, the famed investor and one of the world's richest men, has said that "In looking for someone to hire, you look for three things: integrity, intelligence, and energy. If they don't have the first, the other two kill you." In terms familiar to Berry, Buffett is pointing to the importance of the heart as well as the head and hands. An education of the head and hands will lead to good only if the heart is right. Many people today spend their lives striving desperately to get ahead only to realize that beating everyone else is an empty way of winning. One of life's most important lessons is that there is far more meaning, more satisfaction, and more good to be found in what one gives than in what one gets.

Perhaps this kind of statement sounds a bit old-fashioned to you. Berry emphasizes a moral tradition that is based on service to God, family, and community rather than one built on the spirit of reckless individualism that dominates the world of entertainment and advertising—where grabbing as many toys for yourself as you can is how you win. As Americans, we rightly cherish individual freedoms.

However, it is important to remember that these freedoms occur *within* the context of a moral framework, not outside of one. The rights that we hold as "self-evident" and "unalienable" make sense precisely because they are endowed by a Creator. In other words, we value individuals because we see them as being created in the image of God. Unfettered choice is not a good in and of itself. Choice can be used to promote that which is healthy, good, and right, or it can be used perversely to promote self-indulgence and moral abandonment.

Berry has never been a values-free institution. Of what value is intellectual accomplishment or success in business if it does not lead to a life of conviction, compassion, and courage? At Berry, we want you to develop your intellectual and practical abilities not simply to better yourself, but in a manner consistent with Berry's motto of "not to be ministered unto, but to minister."

Berry's aspiration is that you do something significant with your life, that you choose a path of significance and purpose, one that is of lasting value. This semester, you will participate in a program called *Plan4ward.* Our goal is that you think clearly about what you want to accomplish while at Berry and that you act with intentionality and initiative. We want you to choose goals that are ambitious and meaningful and that combine challenging academic study with meaningful work experiences to foster a sense of direction and seriousness of purpose. We want you to choose a rich variety of experiences by which to explore and develop your interests and talents. That way, the story you tell as you graduate from Berry will be as full of challenge, accomplishment, and inspiration as those of the generations of alumni who preceded you. The path through Berry is still not easy. We have uncommonly high expectations of you. Yet, as Martha Berry once said, "The pursuit of easy things makes us weak. It is the pursuit of the difficult that makes us strong." I look forward to hearing your uncommon and compelling stories four years from now.

College: A Leisurely Corrective to Democracy?

Peter Lawler

Dana Professor of Government and International Studies

Although it may be a bit late to ask, surely you want to know: "What in the world am I doing in college?" You want to improve yourself, and so there must be something about you that needs improving. What you are is determined in some great measure by the way of life of your society. So the question really is: "What's wrong with America?" What are the weaknesses of our way of life that you might want to remedy in yourself?

The best analysis of the strengths and weaknesses of American democracy, *Democracy in America*, was written by Alexis de Tocqueville. Tocqueville was raised as a French aristocrat in the early nineteenth century. But he knew that the days of aristocracy were over and that it was basically good that democracy had defeated it. He thought his job was to view American democracy with a critical eye, to help us be stronger and more free by making us aware of our weaknesses.

The strengths of democracy are powerful and obvious. It is more just than aristocracy. In an aristocracy, rulers come to power on the basis of hereditary right. They need do nothing to deserve to rule. Democracy is based on the principle of equality of opportunity. So there's a closer connection between having power (or wealth) and deserving it. Democracy is also more prosperous than aristocracy. In an aristocracy, the aristocrats don't have to work hard to do well, and those that aren't aristocrats have no incentive to work. In a democracy, everyone works hard because everyone has both the hope of doing well and the fear of losing what he or she has.

A key weakness of democracy is its insufficient appreciation and cultivation of intellectual excellence—artistic, philosophical, and political excellence. Tocqueville observes: "[T]here is no class in America in which a taste for intellectual pleasures is transmitted with hereditary wealth and leisure and which holds the labors of the mind in esteem." Aristocrats are freed up by their social situation from concern with money and power. They have plenty of leisure, which they understand to be for the development of a taste for intellectual pursuits for their own sake. They don't regard the mind mainly as a tool for the production of wealth or power. The pursuit of knowledge is good because it is pleasurable. They have a good time thinking.

Tocqueville describes an American tragedy: "In America, most rich men begin by being poor; almost all men of leisure were busy in their youth; as a result, at the age when one might have a taste for study, one has not the time; and when the time is available, the taste is gone." The Americans, like all people, have a desire to know. But like all desires, it's most powerful when we're young. The American plan is to get rich and then become a person of leisure. The problem is that when the time comes, the American has not developed the taste to fill that leisure with intellectual pleasure. The American tragedy is that we do not know how to use well the leisure that prosperity brings.

One way to understand college is as a remedy to this problem of democracy, a way of keeping your life from being a tragic one. For four years you are, like an aristocrat, freed up to some extent from the pursuits of wealth and power. You may have to work, but only part time, and usually at a friendly Berry job. If you live in the residence halls, many of the necessities of life (cooking, cleaning, etc.) are taken care of by others. You have been given time to exercise your capacity to take pleasure in thought, and at a time in your life when your desire for pleasure is most strong. For a while you will be lucky enough to develop the tastes that will allow you to use your leisure well for the rest of your life. Have a good time.

The Disparity Between Intellect and Character

Robert Coles

Professor of Psychiatry and Medical Humanities at Harvard University

Psychiatrist and Pulitzer Prize-winning author Robert Coles is professor of Psychiatry and medical humanities at Harvard University Medical School and founding editor of Double-Take, a journal of poetry, prose, and photography published by the Center for Documentary Studies at Duke University. In this piece, originally published in the Chronicle of Higher Education, *Coles calls upon students and teachers to act upon the ideals they profess in academic discussions.*

Over 150 years ago, Ralph Waldo Emerson gave a lecture at Harvard University, which he ended with the terse assertion: "Character is higher than intellect." Even then, this prominent man of letters was worried (as many other writers and thinkers of succeeding generations would be) about the limits of knowledge and the nature of a college's mission. The intellect can grow and grow, he knew, in a person who is smug, ungenerous, even cruel. Institutions originally founded to teach their students how to become good and decent, as well as broadly and deeply literate, may abandon the first mission to concentrate on a driven, narrow book learning—a course of study in no way intent on making a connection between ideas and theories on one hand and, on the other, our lives as we actually live them.

Students have their own way of realizing and trying to come to terms with the split that Emerson addressed. A few years ago, a sophomore student of mine came to

Berry students collect funds for the victims of Hurricane Katrina.

see me in great anguish. She had arrived at Harvard from a Midwestern, working-class background. She was trying hard to work her way through college, and, in doing so, cleaned the rooms of some of her fellow students. Again and again, she encountered classmates who apparently had forgotten the meaning of "please", or "thank you"—no matter how high their Scholastic Assessment Test scores—students who did not hesitate to be rude, even crude toward her.

One day she was not so subtly propositioned by a young man she knew to be a very bright, successful pre-med student and already an accomplished journalist. This was not the first time he had made such an overture, but now she had reached a breaking point. She had quit her job and was preparing to quit college in what she called "fancy, phony Cambridge."

The student had been part of a seminar I teach, which links Raymond Carver's fiction and poetry with Edward Hopper's paintings and drawings—the thematic convergence of literary and artistic sensibility in exploring American loneliness, both its social and its personal aspects. As she expressed her anxiety and anger to me, she soon was sobbing hard. After her sobs quieted, we began to remember the old days of that class. But she had some weightier matters on her mind and began to give me a detailed, sardonic account of college life, as viewed by someone vulnerable and hard-pressed by it. At one point, she observed of the student who had propositioned her: "That guy gets all A's. He tells people he's in Group I [the top academic category]. I've taken two moral-reasoning courses with him, and I'm sure he's gotten A's in both of them—and look at how he behaves with me, and I'm sure with others."

She stopped for a moment to let me take that in. I happened to know the young man and could only acknowledge the irony of his behavior, even as I wasn't totally surprised by what she'd experienced. But I was at a loss to know what to say to her. A philosophy major, with a strong interest in literature, she had taken a course on the Holocaust and described for me the ironies she also saw in that tragedy—mass murder of unparalleled historical proportion in a nation hitherto known as one of the most civilized in the world, with a citizenry as well educated as that of any country at the time.

Drawing on her education, the student put before me names such as Martin Heidegger, Carl Jung, Paul De Man, Ezra Pound—brilliant and accomplished men (a philosopher, a psychoanalyst, a literary critic, a poet) who nonetheless had linked themselves with the hate of Nazism and Fascism during the 1930s. She reminded me of the willingness of the leaders of German and Italian universities to embrace Nazi and Fascist ideas, of the countless doctors and lawyers and judges and journalists and school teachers, and, yes, even members of the clergy—who were able to accommodate themselves to murderous thugs because the thugs had political power. She pointedly mentioned, too, the Soviet Gulag, that expanse of prisons to which millions of honorable people were sent by Stalin and his brutish accomplices—prisons commonly staffed by psychiatrists quite eager to label those victims of a vicious totalitarian state with an assortment of psychiatric names, then shoot them up with drugs meant to reduce them to zombies.

I tried hard, toward the end of a conversation that lasted almost two hours, to salvage something for her, for myself, and, not least, for a university that I much respect, even as I know its failings. I suggested that if she had learned what she had just shared with me at Harvard—why, that was itself a valuable education acquired. She smiled, gave me credit for a "nice try," but remained unconvinced. Then she put this tough, pointed, unnerving question to me: "I've been taking all these philosophy courses, and we talk about what's true, what's important, what's good. Well, how do you teach people to be good?" And she added, "What's the point of knowing good, if you don't keep trying to become a good person?"

I suddenly found myself on the defensive, although all along I had been sympathetic to her, to the indignation she had been directing toward some of her fellow students, and to her critical examination of the limits of abstract knowledge. Schools are schools, colleges are colleges, I averred, a complaisant and smug accommodation in my voice. Thereby I meant to say that our schools and colleges these days don't take major responsibility for the moral values of their students, but, rather, assume that their students acquire those values at home. I topped off my surrender to the status quo with a shrug of my shoulders, to which she responded with an unspoken but barely concealed anger. This she expressed through a knowing look that announced that she'd taken the full moral measure of me.

Suddenly, she was on her feet preparing to leave; I realized that I'd stumbled badly. I wanted to pursue the discussion, applaud her for taking on a large subject in a forthright, incisive manner, and tell her she was right in understanding that moral reasoning is not to be equated with moral conduct. I wanted, really, to explain my shrug—point out that there is only so much that any of us can do to affect others' behavior, that institutional life has its own momentum. But she had no interest in that kind of self-justification—as she let me know in an unforgettable aside as she was departing my office: "I wonder whether Emerson was just being 'smart' in that lecture he gave here. I wonder if he ever had any ideas about what to do about what was worrying him—or did he think he'd done enough because he'd spelled the problem out to those Harvard professors?"

She was demonstrating that she understood two levels of irony: One was that the study of philosophy—even moral philosophy or moral reasoning—doesn't necessarily prompt in either the teacher or the student a determination to act in accordance with moral principles. And, further, a discussion of that very irony can prove equally sterile—again carrying no apparent consequences as far as one's everyday actions go.

When that student left my office (she would soon leave Harvard for good), I was exhausted and saddened—and brought up short. All too often those of us who read books or teach don't think to pose for ourselves the kind of ironic dilemma she had posed to me. How might we teachers encourage our students (encourage ourselves) to take that big step from thought to action, from moral analysis to fulfilled moral commitments? Rather obviously, community service offers us all a chance to put our money where our mouths are; and, of course, such service can enrich our understanding of the disciplines we study. A reading of *Invisible Man* (literature), *Tally's Corner* (sociology and anthropology), or *Childhood and Society* (psychology and psychoanalysis) takes on new meaning after some time spent in a ghetto school or a clinic. By the same token, such books can prompt us to think pragmatically about, say, how the wisdom that Ralph Ellison worked into his fiction might shape the way we get along with the children we're tutoring—affect our attitudes toward them, the things we say and do with them.

Yet I wonder whether classroom discussion, per se, can't also be of help, the skepticism of my student notwithstanding. She had pushed me hard, and I started referring again and again in my classes on moral introspection to what she had observed and learned, and my students more than got the message. Her moral righteousness, her shrewd eye and ear for hypocrisy hovered over us, made us uneasy, goaded us.

She challenged us to prove that what we think intellectually can be connected to our daily deeds. For some of us, the connection was established through community service. But that is not the only possible way. I asked students to write papers that told of particular efforts to honor through action the high thoughts we were discussing. Thus goaded to a certain self-consciousness, I suppose, students made various efforts. I felt that the best of them were small victories, brief epiphanies that might otherwise have been overlooked, but had great significance for the students in question.

"I thanked someone serving me food in the college cafeteria, and then we got to talking, the first time," one student wrote. For her, this was a decisive break with her former indifference to others she abstractly regarded as "the people who work on the serving line." She felt that she had learned something about another's life and had tried to show respect for that life.

The student who challenged me with her angry, melancholy story had pushed me to teach differently. Now, I make an explicit issue of the more than occasional disparity between thinking and doing, and I ask my students to consider how we all might bridge that disparity. To be sure, the task of connecting intellect to character is daunting, as Emerson and others well knew. And any of us can lapse into cynicism, turn the moral challenge of a seminar into yet another moment of opportunism: I'll get an "A" this time, by writing a paper cannily extolling myself as a doer of this or that "good deed"!

Still, I know that college administrators and faculty members everywhere are struggling with the same issues that I was faced with, and I can testify that many students will respond seriously, in at least small ways, if we make clear that we really believe that the link between moral reasoning and action is important to us. My experience has given me at least a measure of hope that moral reasoning and reflection can somehow be integrated into students'—and teachers'—lives as they actually live them.

Intellect and Character: Putting Principles Into Action

Consider the courses that you are taking this semester. How many of them require you to consider moral and ethical questions? In the table below, list the courses you are taking and check the box that indicates the frequency of emphasis on moral or intellectual issues:

Course	Moral/ethical issues are never discussed	Moral/ethical issues are discussed occasionally	Moral/ethical issues are discussed daily	Instructor mentions relevant moral issues in lectures	Students are required to take a position on moral or ethical issues.

Choose two or three of the moral principles you are discussing in class that you think are important. How might you honor that principle through action?

1. Moral issue or principle:
   Action:

2. Moral issue or principle:
   Action:

3. Moral issue or principle:
   Action:

Why Study Liberal Arts?

Kathy B. McKee

Associate Provost

Martha Van Cise

Director, Academic Support Center

Just as the depth and strength of a building's foundation determine the height the building can be and how much weight it can support, a liberal-arts education provides the depth of understanding necessary to support advanced study and training. The stronger the foundation, the higher the building or individual can rise. Study of the liberal arts builds the foundation with a well-rounded education in the underlying historical, sociological, artistic, and philosophical contexts of human experience. The liberal-arts education provides the sound education necessary for flexibility in today's rapidly changing world. Just as today's building codes require that structures be built to withstand earthquakes and hurricane-force winds by bending with the forces of nature, the liberal-arts student will be able to shift to meet the demands of an ever-changing work place.

Studying the liberal arts encourages critical thinking and the ability to make discriminating judgments and evaluations by providing myriad experiences in writing, speaking, reasoning, analyzing, and evaluating. These skills equip one with the tools necessary for the successful interpersonal communication so essential in today's diverse community.

The liberal arts provide the background necessary for understanding the specific information and training required for particular fields and disciplines. For instance, in the field of mass communication, certain vocational skills such as news writing, photography, and print and video editing are needed. Yet reporters and editors must have a background in political science, history, economics, sociology, art, and literature to be able to produce clear and accurate material worthy of being edited and distributed. A well-balanced liberal-arts background offers one the foundation on which professional skills can rest.

At Berry, the courses within the general-education curriculum are chosen to help develop such a foundation and to expose students to a breadth of academic disciplines. The goals for the general education are expressed in the College Catalog and should be reflected by the courses within the curriculum:

The courses required for the bachelor's degree at Berry College are designed to assist students in becoming literate, cultured and creative individuals who are also responsible citizens of a democracy in a changing world and who are prepared for lifelong learning. Students will engage in learning that fosters clear and analytical reasoning, effective communication, appreciation of artistic excellence, understanding of scientific and mathematical inquiry, and the ability to make informed and morally responsible choices. They should also acquire that breadth of vision that comes with an historical consciousness and an awareness of cultural and global diversity. The proper cultivation of such a vision emphasizes the best thought and greatest achievement of humankind throughout the course of recorded history.

No matter the vocation or profession followed, liberal-arts studies prepare one for the change and growth inherent in the 21st century. It is the skilled thinkers who have the depth to transcend specific technologies and training and to be retrained as necessary. With a firm foundation in the liberal arts, one learns how to learn and develops the humanity to understand that learning never ends.

Berry College Mission

From the Berry College Strategic Plan 2001–2012

The Berry Mission

Berry College is a comprehensive liberal arts college with Christian values. The college furthers our students' intellectual, moral, and spiritual growth; proffers lessons that are gained from worthwhile work done well; and challenges them to devote their learning to community and civic betterment. Berry emphasizes an educational program committed to high academic standards, values based on Christian principles, practical work experience, and community service in a distinctive environment of natural beauty. It is Berry's goal to make an excellent private liberal-arts education accessible to talented students from a wide range of social and economic backgrounds.

Your College Mission

Drafting a mission statement forces an institution to examine itself, in order to clarify its goals and what it stands for. A thoughtfully composed mission statement that honestly reflects the principles, goals and practices of an institution gives purpose and meaning to the daily work of everyone associated with that institution.

Writing a personal mission statement can likewise help you to clarify goals and behavior and to provide purpose and intention for your actions.

1. **Define yourself.** What adjectives best describe you? How do you want others to see you? What kind of person do you strive to be?

2. **Define your values.** To what ideals are you committed? What do think is most important in life?

3. **State your long term goals**. What do you hope to achieve over the next four years and beyond? Include all areas of your life: educational, familial, social, professional, spiritual.

4. **State how you will fulfill your mission**. Re-examine your goals and values. What will you do to fulfill your goals while staying true to your principles?

5. Review your notes for the four questions above and try to draft a statement no longer than one paragraph. Your mission statement should be easy to understand and remember and should describe what you want to do, who you want to be, and what you will do to meet these goals. Think of this statement as a work in progress. Review it occasionally over the next few months, and revise it as necessary.

MY COLLEGE JOURNEY

Tametria Conner, Class of 2007

I knew coming to college would be a challenging transition for me. I would be 400 miles away from my hometown of Hattiesburg, MS and on my way to adulthood. But I never imagined what a culture shock it would be for me to come from a racially diverse environment to an institution that was 90% Caucasian.

My freshman year was a year of misunderstanding, isolation, and struggle for acceptance. For example, my roommate told me I was "too black,"(whatever that means), that I watched too much BET and that my music was distasteful. She moved out because of these cultural differences. I had never experienced personal racial conflicts similar to this one before coming to Berry. The Caucasian people I interacted with back home never expressed problems with me. It was really a shock to me that people did not accept who I was at Berry.

In addition, I found the social atmosphere very different from my rich culture as an African-American. My freshman year, I was really searching for fun activities and came up short at Berry. Instead of the foam party, BOLD activities, and cosmic bowling, I was expecting stepshows, R&B/Rap concerts, and other culture-specific activities. I had to travel to Atlanta to connect with those activities I enjoy. But all the idle time was converted into studying energy. Because I had nothing to do, I could focus on my academics.

Although I had to struggle in this new system and culture, the struggle helped me transition into my current career as a reporter for WKOT-TV. There are very few minorities in newsrooms across this country, so my experiences at Berry helped prepare me to confront the same challenges that may arise in the newsroom.

Regardless of my cultural experiences at Berry College, I was successful as a student and found ways to get involved. I was a News Producer for Viking Vision Campus News Station, a member of Omicron Delta Kappa National Honor Leadership Society, a Bonner Scholar, and a member and manager of In His Name Gospel Choir, while keeping a 3.58 GPA. In my junior year I attended the IRTS Journalism Workshop in New York and as a senior I traveled with In His Name to the National Association for Collegiate Gospel Choirs conference and was crowned Miss NACGC, a position which has allowed me to help raise awareness about HIV/AIDS among college students.

I think as a minority student at a school like Berry, you have to be strong-willed, strong-minded, have faith in God, and stay focused on what you need to accomplish. You also have to make the choice to keep your identity no matter what happens.

Remember nothing in life is worth getting if you don't struggle.

EFFECTIVE TIME MANAGEMENT

Taming Time

It's a sad but true fact that much of your success or failure in college (and probably the factor that you can control the most) depends directly on how you manage your time. Even though it is such an important factor to master, it is probable that most of us have developed our "time management plan" simply by habit and not by devising a workable action plan. Have you ever stopped to consider that time is one thing in life that can never be saved? It can only be spent, and unfortunately, too many of us have developed the skill of wasting time to a fine art! We may value many things and possessions in life, yet if we had all the money in the world we could not buy one hour. Maybe we should examine this valuable commodity a little more closely!

Why Is Time Management So Crucial?

In high school, it was quite possible to waste fairly large amounts of time without dire consequences. Teachers and parents seemed to give you the benefit of the doubt and understand that you needed some leeway in your time. Even if you've been away from school, you've probably avoided assignments with due dates. But in college, your responsibilities seem to be multiplying in and out of the classroom, and the same habits of "time-waste" will soon catch up with you—possibly with unpleasant results! Many students learn this sad fact too late. Four of the major reasons for dropping out of college have been listed as economic reasons, personal reasons, academic reasons, and lack of organization skills, according to Diana Scharf Hunt—co-author of *Studying Smart: Time Management for College Students*. This lack of organization coupled with a tougher academic load means that time management suddenly becomes (or should become!) a high priority for college students if they are going to be one of the survivors. And that's not even taking into consideration that most college students want to spend some of their time participating in the vast amount of social life available or hold jobs.

Consider the possibility that all of these potential problems can be removed or prevented by the simple realization and acceptance that we frustrate ourselves by trying to control what we can't, and failing to control what we can. Time is the one thing we can never increase. But we can certainly increase our management of it by devising a plan—a workable, personalized, motivating, structuring plan.

What's the Most Important Thing to Learn in College?

Nothing else will be learned unless you learn to control your management of the time available to you. You either control time, or it (or the lack of it) controls you. You must decide. We all have 24 hours in a day—86,400 seconds—to fill up. How do you fill up yours?

Activity:

Take a minute or two to begin filling in "The Week that Was" time schedule. Record what you have accomplished so far today. List your classes, sleeping and eating time, visiting time, dressing time, work time, and, oh yes, your study time! What if this pattern continues for the rest of the week? Continue to record what you do for one week as accurately as possible. Have you controlled time, or did it manipulate you? After you have completed the worksheet, fill in the final portion by analyzing the hours you have spent the past week doing the major necessities of college life—classes, studying, sleeping, eating, and working. Subtract your total from the total amount of hours available in a week, and then divide that by seven to get a daily amount. You may be amazed at the amount of time you waste, or at least fill up with a multitude of things that are not very important.

Where Did It Go?

In a recent study at Southwest Missouri State University, students analyzed their time with these shocking results:

Time spent weekly in class—13 hours
Time spent studying—15 hours
Time spent sleeping—45 hours
Time spent eating—11 hours
Work hours (if they had jobs)—16 hours
Total hours used up—84–100 hours (depending on whether they had a job)
Total hours in a week—168 hours
*Total hours unaccounted for—68–84 hours

That's from 10–14 hours a day! Where does all of that time go? Of course, outside jobs take up some time, and errands, and visiting, and family obligations, etc. . . . But do you have 10 hours today with nothing specific to do? Of course not! No one has that kind of free time—or do they? Is it possible that it's there, and we just can't see it?

For example, did you know that the average American spends seven hours a day watching TV? Even if we said that estimate was much too high and lowered it to 25 hours of TV viewing weekly, that would be 10 years of the average 70-year life—[1/7] of your life in front of a machine! Yet in this same study, the average American only spent 19 minutes daily in active conversation, 13 minutes in hobbies, five minutes in enjoying sports, and four minutes daily in book-reading. These statistics would seem to point to the fact that Americans value TV viewing above all other pastimes, but the study concluded by the participants expressing that they value the other possibilities much more highly than TV. Maybe lack of time is not the problem; maybe it's lack of direction and planning!

The haphazard and careless use of time does at first seem to be much easier and less complicated, but it returns very poor investment dividends. Being organized and controlling your time is much easier in the long run, and less stressful! Remember the value of working smarter, not harder.

Okay, How Do You Control Time?

There are three easy steps in learning to control your time. First, you must have a goal, or you have no purpose to plan. We have discussed the vital importance of goals earlier in this book, but keep in mind that without a goal, you will not know when you have arrived! Secondly, you must formulate a plan to reach that goal—a step-by-step way to get where you want to go. Finally, you must attack your plan and take action. Unfortunately, that's where most of our plans go awry. This is the hardest part, to just get started. We can usually finish if we can just get started! Thomas Huxley once said, "Perhaps the most valuable result of all education is the ability to make yourself do the thing you have to do, when it ought to be done, whether you like it or not." To control time you must take charge of your time by planning your priorities and devising a way to deal with them—one step at a time.

The only way you will ever be able to gain control of your busy schedule is by learning two very simple guidelines.

1. You must learn to do your jobs as efficiently as possible so that they take the least amount of time and still produce the quality of work desired.

2. You must learn to use the small blocks of time usually wasted.

Efficiency experts are frequently hired by large corporations to teach their workers how to produce the most in the least amount of time. Studying should be approached no differently. There are many ways to study more efficiently. Future chapters will provide you some of these ways. As for the second guideline, this is where the 10–14 "lost" hours go for most people—hidden in 18 minute, 10 minute, and four minute intervals. We conveniently convince ourselves that we cannot start, work on, or finish a job now, because we "don't have time." Most projects for busy, productive people cannot be started and finished in one neat, tidy package. It takes distributing the work load in order to finish the task. And that's why you need a time schedule!

What's the Benefit of a Time Schedule?

We'll give you several!

1. *A time schedule saves time.* It takes time to devise a schedule, but it saves time in the long run. This works in much the same way that following a map saves time when traveling. Now you can get from here to there without a map, but it's much more efficient and less stressful to decide on the best route and then follow it!

2. *A time schedule will separate work and play.* It will not rigidly control your life as you may fear, but scheduling will help provide order and discipline. This will free you to work when you work and play when you play. One of the most stressful aspects of college life is that the work never seems to be done. As one

chapter is completed, another is assigned. What's the advantage of taking a test when you just have to start studying for another? If you are going to enjoy your college career and also be successful at it, you must learn to separate work and play. If you don't, your work will not be as efficient as it should be and your play will not be as enjoyable as it could be!

3. *Time schedules reduce the amount of time wasted.* Whether you choose to waste it or not, time has a way of evaporating quickly! For example, did you know that you will spend six months of your life waiting at stop signs? How do you feel about spending eight months of your life opening junk mail, or one whole year looking for lost items? And then there are those five years of waiting in line. If you are going to waste time, you should do the deciding about when to waste it!

4. *Scheduling time helps to decrease your "slacking off" periods.* Most humans tend to slack off in their work habits and productivity near the end of the day, the week, the semester, and so forth. If you plan your schedule you can help to prevent this, or even accommodate this tendency by utilizing your "prime time." This is that time when you are at your peak efficiency and when you can accomplish the most. You won't need to feel guilty about slacking off if you have already achieved your projected plan.

5. *Time schedules help prevent cramming.* If the only benefit of a time schedule was that it helped to prevent cramming and thus promoted retention of learning, we feel it would be worth it! Research after research proves the benefit of distributing your study times into several periods rather than one massive period of torture the night before the test or assignment. Not only will you remember more with this spacing out of studying, but your health and emotional well-being will have a better chance to prosper. Physically as well as academically, cramming does not pay! Just as a path in the woods is more easily seen if traveled over several times, material is more easily recalled if rehearsed at different sessions.

6. *A time schedule helps to promote balance in your life*— a balance of work, study, recreation, and free time. You need breaks as you study (10 minutes for every hour or so is a good rule of thumb), and you need recreation to re-create your body, soul, and spirit. If your balance of life gets out of whack, it is hard to enjoy any aspect of it fully.

7. *Scheduling helps daily chores get accomplished.* By planning it out, maybe you could find a way to manage those chores that seem to get out of hand so easily—things like getting the dishes or the laundry done, writing to your family, or even paying the bills. Schedule a time when you will take care of these little-but-necessary jobs, and half the work is done.

8. *Are you too busy?* One of the greatest benefits of a schedule may be to find out if you CAN get all this stuff done! You may be asking too much of yourself. It simply may not be realistic to work 32 hours a week and take 19 credit hours, plus raise two children (or find time for two boyfriends—whichever fits your situation)! You may find that you must drop certain activities, combine projects, reduce the frequency of events, or alternate weeks in order to live sanely.

9. *Time schedules help you to overcome the worst hurdle of all—getting started!* We tend to avoid the doing of disliked tasks, or substitute doing jobs that are less important, but more appealing. We procrastinate to the best of our ability if it suits our purpose or mood for the moment.

The Problem with Procrastination

If we could learn to solve this problem, most of our time worries would be solved. For most college students, procrastination is the worst academic problem they face, except for the problem of remembering what they have learned. Procrastination seems to be the main cause of anxiety and worry in the overall picture—we could have done a better job and been less stressed out if we had just had more time to do the job! And we could have had more time if we had started the job before the last minute. Procrastination means needlessly postponing tasks until later, and it is really just a strategy that people use to protect themselves from certain fears. These fears usually involve the fear of failing, or even succeeding! Statements like: "I must be perfect," "It's safer to do nothing than do the wrong thing," or "If I do a good job, I may have to do an even better job next time" are common thoughts for procrastinators. Many of us probably fall into this category if we are honest with ourselves. Overcoming procrastination is a matter of habit and will-power, and the only way to cure the problem is to face the fears. Setting daily goals, prioritizing, breaking the job into small, easily-accomplished sub-parts, setting time limits, and rewarding yourself for an accomplished task may help you with the procrastination problem.

How Do You Make a Time Schedule?

You will first need to consider what type of time schedule or schedules will best suit your purposes. There are daily schedules, weekly schedules, or semester schedules, and you may need one or all of these. As a suggested minimum, you will need a semester calendar, an average weekly master plan, and a daily list. If you want the maximum of efficiency, you need to incorporate all three types of schedules.

The Semester Calendar

As soon as you get your different class syllabi for a new semester, you should fill out as much of a semester calendar as you can. Plot test dates, due dates, (VACATION DATES!), and begin to develop an overall scheme of busy weeks versus planning weeks. You might even plot in notes to yourself like "Start worrying about term paper topic" or "Two tests coming up in two weeks" on your calendar at the appropriate locations. You will begin to feel a little more in control as soon as your calendar is in shape. Now all you have to do is plan on how to accomplish the week-by-week tasks.

The Weekly Master Plan

Let's now work on making a weekly schedule for an average week in your current semester. On the Master Time Schedule provided, you should first schedule in the names of the classes you are taking. Attending class may not be your only "job" right now, but it should certainly be a very high priority if you are going to be successful in college. In a very real aspect, attending class is your career right now. Do it professionally!

Secondly, go back through the time schedule and list those demands on your time that do not vary that much from week to week. You might call this "Necessary Time." It would include such things as outside jobs, eating, sleeping, clubs, sports, practices, commuting time, church, housekeeping chores, etc.

After having filled in CLASS TIME and NECESSARY TIME, you are now ready to figure out STUDY TIME. In order to accomplish this task, you should first analyze your study time from "The Week That Was" Time Schedule you filled out. Take a minute to complete the Time Analyzer Worksheet before you go any further and then decide how you measure up. You should try to remediate problems that you are giving yourself by your study behavior. Remember, your goal is to study smarter, not harder. The step of deciding WHAT to study WHEN will be one of the most important decisions you will make this semester. We'll look at this carefully in the next section.

Finally, the blank spaces that will remain in your time schedule after you fill in your study time will be your FREE TIME. We usually can find plenty of ways to fill in these blanks as the days go by. The problem that must now be dealt with is how to schedule that study time.

How Do I Decide When to Study?

In the first place, you need to decide how much time is needed for study. In high school, 15–30 minutes per class was usually sufficient, but those days are gone! Usually a 2/1 ratio is suggested—that is, two hours of study for every hour of class time. So a very general rule would be that if you were carrying 15 credit hours, you should find 30 hours of study time. Of course, some classes might not require this, but some may require more. It is much wiser to plan too much time and not need it than to not plan enough and find out too late just how badly it was needed! Usually a one hour study session with a ten minute break could be a workable goal for most students. You would need to adapt this to what is most productive for you; 30- or 45-minute slots with five minute breaks might be more beneficial.

As to how to pick the most productive time to study each subject, consider these guidelines.

1. The OPTIMUM TIME for the most efficiency is usually RIGHT AFTER THE CLASS. To study the subject right BEFORE THE CLASS meets can be very advantageous for discussion classes, or even just a quick review of notes before a lecture can make those classes more beneficial. To pick a time slot right after class can increase your efficiency and decrease the time needed to study. For example, a 30-minute study immediately after class could be worth one hour of study later. You tend to be more interested in the subject at that time, need less warm-up time to get involved in the studying, and there tends to be less confusion about assignments if they are started quickly.

2. Try planning a time to REVIEW your notes immediately BEFORE YOU GO TO SLEEP. Plan on learning new material when you are fresh, but review right before you retire. Studies have shown that you retain this reviewed material better if you sleep on it. In fact, the shorter the delay between study and bed, the more likely you are to retain the material!

3. Plan on studying your MOST DIFFICULT CLASSES IN THE EARLY AFTERNOON, for the most part. Long-term memory seems to be more effective then, as well as hand-eye coordination and physical strength. If you need to memorize or juggle words or figures, your short-term memory is more effective in the morning, so plan those types of activities for earlier hours. Beware of general low-energy time zones—for most people these center around 2–5 pm (when neural functions decline and blood sugar levels are lower) or 2–7 AM (when

most accidents that can be attributed to human error occur). These might not be the optimum times to write that difficult research paper.

4. FOLLOW YOUR BIOLOGICAL CLOCK. Find your prime times and work with your body rather than fighting against its natural tendencies. To find whether you are a night person (an owl) or a morning person (a lark), take the inventory and then plan to study for tests at your peak periods. Morning people tend to jump out of bed early in the morning with a drive to have a productive morning. They tend to lead controlled, structured, well-regulated lives. They begin to slow down about mid-afternoon and believe and follow the old adage of "Early to bed, early to rise . . ."

On the other hand, night people (or owls) crawl rather than jump out of bed, barely survive mornings, begin to wake up about noon and become their normally extroverted selves, peak in mid-afternoon, and wind down quite a bit later. No one tendency is the correct one, but you must work with your preference or it will defeat you. Don't plan on getting up early and cramming for the big final if you are a night owl. You probably won't make it up! And if you are a morning lark, you'd better not go ahead and attend the big party with lofty plans to study all night long. Your body won't make things easy for you to follow through with your plans. Consider these factors when you schedule classes.

One final thought about your body's biological clock is that most people tend to find benefit in keeping in step with the sun. There seems to be some added benefits to working during daylight hours and resting during night hours.

5. Make sure you SPACE YOUR STUDYING PROPERLY. Remember to plan and use breaks that vary greatly from what your study activity was. Alternate different types of study activities. For example, plan to study an activity subject (such as math or composition) between subjects that require a lot of reading. And make sure you space out the studying required for each subject. It will usually be more effective to study biology in three one-half hour sessions rather than a single one and one-half hour session. Don't forget to include a time to review past notes also. Otherwise, you will be practically starting over when it is time for testing.

6. DOUBLE TIME ESTIMATES AS YOU PLAN. Things always seem to take longer than originally thought. In fact, you need to guard against "Parkinson's Law"—work always stretches to fill whatever time is available. Instead of planning on studying one hour, plan how much you will get accomplished in one hour. Set goals and limits and you will be able to achieve more.

7. Plan to STUDY EACH SUBJECT AT THE SAME TIME, ON THE SAME DAYS, AND IN THE SAME PLACE (one place with everything you need close at hand). Again, the idea is to work with your body instead of against it, and you can condition your body to not resist studying so much if you establish very firm habits. If you have psychology on Mondays, Wednesdays, and Fridays, the best time to study would be on those days at whatever time you designate would fit your biological clock, your time schedule, and be closest to psychology class time.

8. In general, plan to study the WORST FIRST, EASIEST (OR MORE INTERESTING) LAST. Prioritize, and then plan on getting the tough stuff over while your energy and initiative are at their peaks.

What about "Daily" Time Management?

As you try to follow your weekly Master Time Schedule, you will also need to make daily plans. A good suggestion is to make out this daily plan before you go to bed at night. Although it takes time and energy, devising a list of what you would like to accomplish the next day will help give you direction and purpose, and start your day more efficiently. But one more step is needed—prioritize that list before you start sawing logs. That way if you don't get everything done you will at least have accomplished the most important things. Try making some copies of the Daily Plan Worksheet we've provided, and see if it doesn't help you to put life into perspective and order. You're beginning to get a grip on it!

CRITICAL THINKING

Take a minute to look back on yesterday's events. Write down all the things that you did yesterday—in the order that you did them. Analyze your accomplishments. Did you think about the priority of the task as you started to work? Did you really accomplish the things that needed to be taken care of yesterday? Would there have been a better order to have worked on those tasks, or should some tasks have been omitted and others substituted? Try prioritizing yesterday's events now in the light of a new day. If you had worked in this order yesterday, would today's tasks be any easier or more organized? Keep this activity in mind as you think about whether to make a list and prioritize it for tomorrow!

Any Other Time Management Tips?

Sure! Take a look at these:

1. Make studying as portable as possible. Carry pocket work/note cards to study when you are on the go.

2. Use those small blocks of time usually wasted. Recite, review, and plan in-between classes, while waiting in lines, etc. Carry a small notepad to help you plan.

3. Make lists and prioritize them. This idea paid one man (efficiency expert Ivy Lee) $25,000 and made Bethlehem Steel Company and Charles Schwab, its president, a hundred million dollars! Lee instructed each steel worker to make a list each day, prioritize the list, and then work on the first item until it was done. Then, and only then, they were to move on to the second item. This strategy turned that little known company into the biggest independent steel producer in the world. The idea was simple then, and is still simply effective now—take things one at a time in their proper order.

4. Recognize four things that will steal more time from you than you can make up for—laziness, sidetracks, procrastination, and day-dreaming. These things must constantly be fought.

5. Use calendars, clocks, appointment books, and notepads to their full advantage by planning ahead, organizing, and following the plan.

6. Try to handle each task only once. Finish the job as much as your schedule will allow before proceeding to the next task.

7. Practice trading time, not stealing it. Has an unexpected social event popped up? Go ahead and attend guilt-free—as long as you trade the study time you had planned for free time later in your schedule. Don't just put it off—plan and trade it.

8. Learn to say no, and mean it.

9. Control interruptions.

10. Avoid perfectionism. Shoot for your best, but don't overdo this time-sapper.

11. Plan, and then start! Remember: the more time spent planning, the less time needed to accomplish the task. When it's time to start the task, throw yourself into it with enthusiasm. Don't wait for inspiration to strike. It probably won't. Don't inch into the water—dive in! Genuine enthusiasm may follow!

Mastering the Time Trap

Now that you know why to do it, and how to do it, let's do it! Devise your master time schedule and diligently attempt to follow it. You may soon find that there are a lot of benefits in being the master OF—rather than being mastered BY—your time. You can win in the game of time if you learn what the worn-out, frustrated student in this example learned:

"I can't keep our appointment," he sighed. "I find myself swamped. It's getting to be too much!"

"You've contracted a malady about as unique as the common cold," replied his friend. "It's called Wrong Ending. You know, we were all given two ends to use. On one we sit, with one we muse. Success depends on which we use . . . heads you win, tails you lose."

One final comment—don't forget the importance of balance in your life. Does your time schedule have a balance of work and play, study and recreation? Get your life too much out of balance in either direction and you are asking for trouble. You're on your way to a bright future if you learn the secret of mastering your time! And what a secret to learn, for the waste of time is one price winners can't afford to pay!

Summary

In this chapter we have discussed the fact that it is critical to master time management in college in order to succeed academically AND socially. College students are very busy people with places to go, family obligations, people to see, and tests for which to study! None of these things can happen efficiently unless one learns to control the balance of work and play in his life. Effective people must also learn to work out a manageable way to arrange their schedule so that they are making the best use of the time they have. Lack of time is really not the problem; procrastination and poor planning are the real culprits. We learn to control time by devising and learning to follow a time schedule that takes into consideration our schedules, goals, priorities, and biological make-up. The benefits of this planning device are numerous, including distributing the work load and helping to reduce stress. This chapter has given you an opportunity to make a time schedule and suggestions for choosing your optimum study times. There are ways to make time management more efficient and effective, and the suggestions included in the last section of the chapter should give you some positive steps to take in the right direction!

QUICK TIP

Get To Know The Library

If you think of the library as a silent and dusty repository of outdated information, think again. Memorial Library is home to over 700,000 print and microform volumes. It subscribes to more than 2000 journals and magazines and is equipped with a coffee shop, Wi-Fi, laptop docking and computer stations, 400 individual study seats and group study areas. Open 105 hours a week, with knowledgeable friendly staff on call to assist with finding information of all sorts, the library is a convenient place to catch up on work or email between classes and provides a comfortable alternative to studying in a residence hall.

For more information on the library, see Reading 7

Hours Per Week Berry Freshman Spent in Online Social Networks (i.e Facebook, My Space)

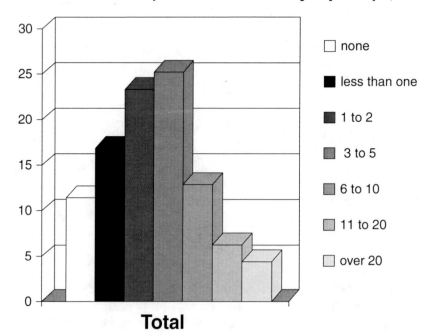

"The Week That Was": Your Current Time Schedule

	Monday	Tuesday	Wednesday	Thursday	Friday	Saturday	Sunday
6:00 A.M.							
7:00 A.M.	Wake	Wake	Wake	Wake	Wake	Wake	Wake
8:00 A.M.	Breakfst	Class	Break	Class	Break		
9:00 A.M.	Class	Work	Class	Work	Class		
10:00 A.M.	↓	│	│	│	│		
11:00 A.M.	Work	│	Work	│	Work		
noon	↓	↓	│	↓	│		
1:00 P.M.	Class	Class	Class	Class	│		
2:00 P.M.	↓		↓	Voice	Class		
3:00 P.M.	Class		Class		Class		
4:00 P.M.	Class	Class	Class	Class			
5:00 P.M.							
6:00 P.M.							
7:00 P.M.							
8:00 P.M.							
9:00 P.M.							
10:00 P.M.							
11:00 P.M.							
midnight							
1:00 A.M.							
2:00 A.M.							

Totals:

Hours Spent in Class   18

Hours Spent Studying   3

Hours Spent Sleeping   6

Hours Spent Eating   3

Hours Spent Working   16

Total

168 (total hours in one week)

–

(Your total "necessary hours")

Hours uncommitted weekly

Time Analyzer for "The Week That Was" Worksheet

Analyze your current time usage by answering these questions based on what is normal for you.

	YES	NO
1. I often study at a time when I am not at peak efficiency due to fatigue.	_____	_____
2. I have failed to complete at least one assignment on time this semester.	_____	_____
3. This week I spent time watching TV, visiting, or napping that really should have been spent otherwise.	_____	_____
4. Often, lack of prioritizing tasks causes me some difficulty in completing tasks on time.	_____	_____
5. Social or athletic events cause me to neglect academic work fairly often.	_____	_____
6. At least once this semester, I have not remembered that an assignment was due until the night before.	_____	_____
7. I often get behind in one course due to having to work on another.	_____	_____
8. I usually wait until the night before the due date to start assignments.	_____	_____
9. My studying is often a hit-or-miss strategy which is dependent on my mood.	_____	_____
10. I normally wait until test time to read texts and/or review lecture notes.	_____	_____
11. I often have the sinking realization that there is simply not enough time left to accomplish the assignment or study sufficiently for the test.	_____	_____
12. Often I rationalize that very few people will make the A/get the project done on time/really read the text, etc.	_____	_____
13. I catch myself looking forward to study interruptions rather than trying to avoid them.	_____	_____
14. I have failed to eliminate some time wasters this past week that I could have controlled.	_____	_____
15. I often feel out of control in respect to time.	_____	_____
16. I have procrastinated at least twice this week.	_____	_____
17. I find myself doing easier or more interesting tasks first, even if they are not as important.	_____	_____
18. I feel I have wasted quite a lot of time—again—this week.	_____	_____
19. I studied EACH course I am currently taking this week.	_____	_____
20. I spent some time this week reviewing previous weeks' notes even though I did not have a test.	_____	_____
21. The time of day that I am the most alert is _____, so I tried to study my hardest subjects then.	_____	_____
22. I studied approximately 1–2 hours out of class for every hour in class.	_____	_____

	YES	NO

23. My most sluggish period during the day is _____, so I used these times to relax or participate in sports or hobbies.   _____ _____

24. I often make out daily lists of tasks to be completed, and I prioritize these lists.   _____ _____

25. I use small blocks of time (10–30 min.) between classes to review notes, start assignments, or plan.   _____ _____

To calculate your score, score 1 point for each yes from items 1–18, and 1 point for each no from items 19–25. The higher your score, the more you need a Master Time Schedule! Consider these categories for your score:

15–19 YOU'RE IN DESPERATE NEED OF A PLAN! How do you ever get anything accomplished? (Or do you?)

10–14 YOU NEED A PLAN! Life could be simpler if you took the time to plan it out.

5–9 A PLAN WOULD HELP! The going could be smoother, and more could be accomplished.

0–4 A PLAN COULDN'T HURT! You're doing pretty well, but give yourself the gift of organization, and you may give yourself the gift of more time.

Please write a paragraph that reflects on your results.

Master Time Schedule

	Monday	Tuesday	Wednesday	Thursday	Friday	Saturday	Sunday
6:00 A.M.							
7:00 A.M.							
8:00 A.M.							
9:00 A.M.							
10:00 A.M.							
11:00 A.M.							
noon							
1:00 P.M.							
2:00 P.M.							
3:00 P.M.							
4:00 P.M.							
5:00 P.M.							
6:00 P.M.							
7:00 P.M.							
8:00 P.M.							
9:00 P.M.							
10:00 P.M.							
11:00 P.M.							
midnight							
1:00 A.M.							
2:00 A.M.							

Morning Lark vs. Night Owl

This questionnaire can help you determine if you are a morning person (a lark) or a night person (an owl). "Larks" usually lead well-structured, controlled lives. They jump out of bed and usually have productive mornings, tending to wind down about mid-afternoon. "Owls," on the other hand, tend to crawl out of bed, barely live through mornings, but have more productive afternoons. They also tend to be more extroverted than larks. Which are you? Find out by circling the answer most appropriate for you and adding up your points.

	Points Possible	Points Earned
1. I feel best if I get up around:		_____
5–6:30 AM	5	
6:30–7:30 AM	4	
7:30–9:30 AM	3	
9:30–11 AM	2	
11–noon	1	
2. If I had to describe how easy it is for me to get up in the morning, I would say:		_____
It is not easy at all!	1	
It is not very easy.	2	
It is fairly easy.	3	
It is very easy.	4	
3. The way I feel for the first half-hour after I wake up is:		_____
very tired	1	
fairly tired	2	
fairly refreshed	3	
very refreshed	4	
4. If I could choose the best time to take a difficult test, it would be:		_____
8–10 AM	4	
10 am–1 PM	3	
1–5 PM	2	
7–9 PM	1	
5. If my job would require that I work from 4–6 AM one day, I would choose to:		_____
not go to bed until after I worked	1	
take a nap before and sleep after	2	
sleep before work and nap after	3	
get all the sleep I need before work	4	

	Points Possible	Points Earned
6. If someone asked me to jog with them at 7 AM one morning, I would perform:		_____
well	4	
reasonably well	3	
not very well	2	
not well at all	1	
7. If I have to wake up at a specific time each morning, I depend on my alarm clock:		_____
not at all	4	
slightly	3	
quite a lot	2	
desperately	1	
8. I am usually tired and wanting to go to bed by:		_____
8–9 PM	5	
9–10:30 PM	4	
10:30 pm–12:30 AM	3	
12:30–2 AM	2	
2–3 AM	1	

TOTAL NUMBER OF POINTS EARNED _____

A score of 20 is halfway between owl and lark. The higher your score, the more of a morning lark you are. The lower your score, the more of a night owl you are.

Daily Plan for _____

Jobs to Complete	Due Date	Priority	Completed?
1. _____			
2. _____			
3. _____			
4. _____			
5. _____			
6. _____			
7. _____			
8. _____			
9. _____			
10. _____			

Phone Calls to Make			
1. _____			
2. _____			
3. _____			
4. _____			

Errands to Run	Due Date	Priority	Completed?
1. _____			
2. _____			
3. _____			
4. _____			
5. _____			
6. _____			

People to See			
1. _____			
2. _____			
3. _____			
4. _____			

Notes to Myself

UNIT 2

GETTING YOUR BEARINGS

INTRODUCTION

To take one's bearings means, literally, to determine one's position with regard to one's surroundings. Obviously, the more familiar the surroundings, the easier it is to get your bearings. Think about your room at home. You probably know its layout so well that you could cross from point to point with your eyes shut. Now remember the last time you woke up in an unfamiliar room. It probably took you a moment to remember where you were; you had to get your bearings before you could even determine which side of the bed to get out of.

As a new college student, you may find it difficult to get your bearings. You are getting to know not only a new campus, but new people and a new way of living as well. And many of the guides on whom you depended in the past (parents, teachers, siblings, friends), are not close by to help you.

The readings in this unit are intended to help you get oriented to this new literal and metaphorical place. Reading 3 examines the personal and social landscape new college students face, from getting along with roommates to managing money. The essays in Reading 4 deal with the new and often uncomfortable intellectual climate of college. This new place in which you find yourself is not just "college," but more specifically Berry College, so in Reading 5 you'll read about the history and traditions of this unique institution.

What Kind of Place Have I Gotten Myself Into?

Debbie Heida

Dean of Students

So, you're here. And now you begin to live the life of a college student. In those times during your senior year that you weren't busily involved in school work, church group, choir, band, athletics, volunteering in your community, or helping your family, you probably had some time to think about what college life would be like. And over the next several months, you will have many experiences that match those expectations and some that do not. Our minds are wonderful places to create, to dream, to hope, and to imagine. But as with any experience that we imagine, reality is somewhat different.

Some time ago, Ernest Boyer of the Carnegie Foundation for the Advancement of Teaching, described six principles of the communities we aim to be. These principles operate in tandem, with the whole being more than the sum of the parts. Our college community is:

1. *An educationally purposeful community.* Both in and out of the classroom, in the lab and at your work site, on the athletic field or in the residence, this campus is a learning lab where students, faculty and staff both learn and teach. That's our goal—to learn and grow with you.

2. *An open community.* A campus is a place to explore ideas and values and wrestle with the ones that will have the most meaning for you. Freedom of speech,

oral or written, is uncompromisingly protected here. But equally as strong is our commitment to respectful discourse, where ideas are debated and the persons respected. Until the late 1960's, our student handbook stated "A Berry student is never rude." We are not so explicit in our rules today but our expectation of respect is firmly part of Berry.

3. *A just community.* Each person is a valued member of our Berry community. Varied backgrounds and interests and diverse experiences are a valuable part of our campus. Our community includes diverse cultures, ethnicities, gender, sexual orientation, religious and political convictions, the list could go on.

4. *A disciplined community.* The rights you've dreamed of as you become an adult—they're here. The responsibility to make good choices, to do no harm to your community and to take an active role in the governance of your campus, that's here, too.

5. *A caring community.* We care deeply about who you become and what your experiences here are all about. We have many resources in place to help you when you're homesick or struggling with preparing for your first exam. There are faculty and staff who are prepared to celebrate your success on your first research paper, to support you through the break up of your first serious relationship or your success in finding your life partner.

6. *A celebrative community.* We are proud of the 104 year history of Berry College. We have wonderful traditions (Mountain Day, mud wrestling, formals, Agriculture Week, etc.) that celebrate our proud heritage as a college. We also create new traditions every year (plan to attend Marthapalooza the Saturday night following Mountain Day).

This community will feel like home at different points for different students. For some students, it feels like home only after going home for the Christmas holidays and realizing that you're anxious to come back, see your friends here, and get started in classes again. For others, it feels like home almost immediately. And for some of you, it may take figuring out what major is right for you and mapping a career direction in order to truly feel a part of Berry. While each of the principles describes our campus as a whole, they only come alive through you — your active participation in the classroom, in student organizations, in your resident halls, at your work site, in your volunteer activities in the community, in the dining hall at Krannert, in Dana and East Mary and Morton-Lemley during late night conversation.

These are great ideals, but does this mean I'm going to like this place? One of our most famous presidents, Abraham Lincoln, once said, "Most people are about as happy as they make up their minds to be." Your potential is great; our admissions office acted on that potential some months ago. Now it's up to you. There will be highs and lows to your Berry experience just as there have been to most of the experiences that have had great meaning in your life to date. The rest of the Berry community is committed to a kind of teaching and learning that is unique to Berry. We look forward to the impact you will make here.

Works Cited

Boyer, Ernest L. "Campus Life In Search of Community," The Carnegie Foundation for the Advancement of Teaching, 1990.

My College Journey

John Hall, Class of 2009

When I came to Berry College in the fall of 2004, I was a typical student in an atypical situation. I had been in a cheerleading accident and left wheelchair-bound only a year ago and I was still getting used to my injury. During the Viking Venture there was an activity where we had to stand on a tarp and turn it over without anyone step-ping off. My first thought was that there was no way I could get this done. I told my group I would be willing to sit out the activity, but they would not hear of it. We finished the activity with me on the tarp, and it really felt good to fit in somewhere again.

As a freshman, I dealt with the same problems as everyone else, but to a different extent. One of the hardest adjustments was having to depend on people for everyday things. Before my accident, I was very independent. I liked to get things done myself and take responsibility for my own work. It embarrassed me to ask people to open the door or grab a book for me, which led me to become very introverted. But I soon found out that everyone can use help in college. The Academic Support Center provides accommodations to students with a variety of needs and tutors in every subject. A good tutor can be the difference between a C and an A. So don't be afraid to seek help if you need it.

Like many new students, I learned quickly the importance of being organized, something I had never mastered before. My mom was a teacher at the middle school I attended and literally cleaned out my locker when I couldn't fit anything else in it. I used to turn in English work in Algebra folders, and it all just looked like a stack of thrown together papers. After my injury, I was unable to write, so I did all my work on a computer. That made it a little easier to stay organized. I also learned to organize more in my head. I started using pneumonic devices to improve my memory. My greatest feat in college, however, was organizing my time. For me to survive in college I had to get a routine. Since I can not use my hands to switch books, I can only really study when I have help. So I try my hardest to plan ahead.

No matter how much planning ahead I did, nothing prepared me for what happened my first semester. I was sick a lot of the time, while trying to find the time to write about two papers a week. I came to Berry with a steady girlfriend of 10 months. When we argued, my grades suffered. In the middle of my first semester things seemed to fall apart. I had developed a severe pressure sore that forced me to miss two weeks of class. At that point, I began to wonder if a traditional college was right for me. I thought maybe I should pursue my degree online. I was on the verge of dropping my classes when my mom, who is the strongest person I know, told me to quit pitying myself and get my work done because without a college education I would have nothing. We worked about five hours a day for two weeks and I finished the semester with three A's and three B's.

Now, I am a senior and applying to law school. I have fought sickness, been through a hard breakup, participated in Model U.N., and written more papers on more topics than I can remember. Whatever challenges lie ahead, I'll just put on my pants one leg at a time and tell life to bring it on.

How Not to Lose a Roommate in 15 Weeks:
What You Need to Know to Make it Work

Lindsey Taylor
Director of Residence Life

The biggest mistake that roommates make is that instead of just telling the other person what they're mad about, they do something to get even. . .so then everybody's mad and it just snowballs.
Junior (RA), Engineering, University of Miami

Like all things new, there comes a point when the "new" wears off and "old" sets in. The same is true with roommates. The first day of move-in is exciting! You and your roommate have rearranged the room half a dozen times trying to maximize your space, you have both rolled your eyes a dozen times at your parents and their crazy suggestions, and as soon as they leave, the two of you vow to have the best freshman year ever!

Or maybe your first day of move-in was not as exciting. Your roommate could care less about maximizing space, he or she thought it was lame that your parents came to help you move in, and after your parents left, and you sat on your bed wondering "What have I gotten myself into?"

Being a roommate means more than just sharing space for the next nine months. You may be best friends or you may never see each other outside your room. Either way, you are learning about setting boundaries, communicating openly, and exploring new freedoms. Learning to live with a roommate takes patience, understanding, a sense of humor, but most importantly, communication and compromise.

Though we frequently hear of their importance, communication and compromise can be hard in practice. Effective communication is more than leaving a Post-It note on your computer with the instructions "DO NOT USE" written with hopes your roommate will get the hint. Though your roommate will get the message loud and clear, your roommate is left wondering what he/she did to make you leave the note. A better, more effective way to communicate with your roommate is by using "I" statements. For example, try saying, "I would feel better about your using my computer if you would ask first, and I will do the same when I would like to use/borrow your things." Using "I" statements will prevent putting your roommate on the defensive. Be honest with your roommate about how you feel, but remember none of us are perfect. When trying to communicate, create a neutral zone. Do not attack your roommate as soon as he or she walks into the room, wait until your emotions have calmed down, and then if necessary, ask your roommate to talk with you over a cup of coffee or something to eat. Sometimes addressing roommate issues in the room only generates more conflict. By removing yourselves from the place of tension, you are more likely to communicate openly and honestly without distractions or reminders of irritations.

Three Key Steps to Effective Communication:

1. *Remove Yourself:* wait to address a conflict until your emotions are not running high. Remove yourself from the situation, collect your thoughts, and then address the conflict/issue when you can talk objectively and not emotionally.

2. *Neutral Zone:* go somewhere private and unintimidating to discuss problems. Going to eat a meal or grabbing a cup of coffee is a great way to create a neutral zone.

3. *Be Honest:* tell your roommate how you really feel while you have their attention. However, remember to use "I" statements to avoid attacking your roommate—none of us is perfect.

Now that you know how to effectively communicate with your roommate, how do you resolve a conflict by compromising? Finding a compromise does not mean getting your roommate to see things or do things your way. Compromise is finding a middle ground that is acceptable to both you and your roommate. In order for a compromise to be successful, all parties involved must be willing to give and take. However, stand up for yourself. Do not let your roommate dictate the expectations of the room, but rather brainstorm with each other to find ways that you can both be happy in the room. Having a roommate means you may have to adjust to each other's needs. For example, if you come into the room at 2 a.m. and your roommate is asleep, get ready for bed quickly and quietly. If your roommate is studying for an exam or writing a paper in the room, make your telephone calls elsewhere. If you show your roommate respect with little actions, finding compromise with bigger issues will not be as difficult.

Three Key Steps to Successful Compromise:

1. *Be Willing:* you must be willing to give and take when formulating a compromise.

2. *Stand Up:* do not be afraid to stand up for yourself. Express concerns while you and your roommate are brainstorming options, but don't forget to use "I" statements!

3. *Show Respect:* your roommate will appreciate that you show respect with little actions. Having respect for each other will strengthen your relationship.

The next four years will be unique to anything you may ever experience. Your tenure at Berry College should challenge you to grow academically and socially.

Students bring their families, cultures, experiences, beliefs, values, and expectations to college with them. Living in the Residence Halls will allow you to explore others' backgrounds and experiences. Your exploration could result in confirming your own beliefs, values, and morals, or it could challenge your own beliefs, values, and morals. Either way, developing empathy and an awareness for others can enhance the relationships you form while at Berry College as well as beyond the Gate of Opportunity. Do not be afraid to ask questions of others, but be prepared to listen fully to their answers. Before casting judgment or formulating an opinion, reflect on what you hear—you may gain valuable insight.

Relationships of any kind are challenging and require patience as well as a willingness to learn about the other. Some of the best roommate pairs have been those who have opposing viewpoints but respect each other's opinions. Remember, you are not in this alone. If talking with your roommate is not helping, seek advice and/or help from your Resident Assistant. The Director, Assistant Director, and Coordinator for Residence Life as well as counselors in the Counseling Center want to help make your time at Berry successful, and are willing to help you maintain healthy relationships.

You don't have to hang out with him, you don't have to like him, but you do have to RESPECT him.
Junior, History, Notre Dame

QUICK TIP

Form A Study Group

Regularly studying with two or three other students in your class can be effective for several reasons. You will be accountable to the group, which will motivate you to come to study sessions prepared. If you are having difficulty grasping a difficult concept, chances are someone in the group will be able to clarify it for you. You'll also benefit from the opportunity to explain concepts to others; teaching is one of the best paths to true learning. A study group can widen your network of friends too, although it's important that the group stay focused on the work during designated study times. *For more on developing good study habits, see Reading 9.*

Roommate Case Studies

The incidents below are based on the real experiences of Berry students. Choose one, and complete the worksheet on the back of this page.

1. You and your roommate really hit it off when you first move into your dorm. You have many similar interests and plenty of things to talk about. You have agreed to share snacks and drinks, and your roommate brought a mini fridge. A few weekends into the semester, you decide to drive home to visit your family and your roommate stays on campus. When you return Sunday afternoon, you notice some of your clothes on the floor near your roommate's bed. You also notice your shower caddy is much less organized than you left it. When you confront your roommate, he doesn't admit to using your things, but observes that since you are sharing his fridge, he assumed that meant he was entitled to use your things, too.

2. After a busy day, you decide to go to bed early. Around 3AM, you wake up to find your roommate and his/her significant other making out on your roommate's bed. You know that they are violating visitation hours, and you are very uncomfortable with their make-out session just a few feet away from you.

3. You ask to borrow your roommate's calendar, and he/she tells you it is in the closet. When you open your roommate's closet, you see a rather large stash of alcohol. Not only is your roommate under age, but you know that it is against Berry policy to have alcohol in dorm rooms.

4. Starting the first day of Viking Venture, you awake to your roommate getting ready. She has turned on all the lights and has been using her hair dryer for a good 20 minutes. And, it is 6:30AM. You turn to her from your bed and ask her how long she'll be. She says she still has to curl her hair and do her makeup. Every day since then, the routine has been the same: lights on at 5:30 AM and the hairdryer at 6, even though she has nowhere to be for another two hours. You just want to get a little more sleep.

Case Study Worksheet

State the problem, issue or question that needs to be resolved.

What is at stake for each party?

List several ways that the problem might be resolved.

Write down the best way to solve the problem and why you would solve it that way.

My College Journey

Viraj Deshmukh

American Pie, Van Wilder, Revenge of the Nerds, Eurotrip: Such movies were my only source of information about what American college life was supposed to be like. I remember sitting in the Boeing 747 in July 2006, getting ready to take off from Mumbai, India, for the United States, and wondering whether I would be able to adapt to the not-so-familiar lifestyle of "sex, drugs, and alcohol" that I assumed I would find in my new school: Berry College.

Transitioning from high school to college is tough enough; I had to transition from one continent to another. Getting used to the food, the climate, and the methods of studying was a painstaking process but socializing was the toughest part of my struggle. Learning distinctively American colloquialisms like "What's up" took me a while. The dry sarcasm and one-liners used in the English language were much different than the humor that I was used to in India. There were times when everybody around me was laughing at a joke and I had no clue whatsoever about what was going on.

Thankfully, during this struggle of mine, I discovered that Berry was not the stereotypical heartless university I had expected. In fact, it was the most loving and accepting culture that I had ever been in. I quickly learned that it was quite simple to make friends at Berry and I drafted out a few guidelines that might help other new students, even those closer to home:

1. Introduce yourself.

2. Remember names and a distinctive feature (likes video games, football etc.).

3. Smile and always say hi.

4. And more importantly, be yourself and learn to love others. Remember that there will always be a few people who love you for what you are. All you have to do is love them back.

Campus Activities— More Than Just Fun!

Cecily Crow

Director of Student Activities

All students come to college with one thing in common—everyone has 168 hours a week to fill. What differs is how you choose to use those hours. Of course, there are certain basic necessities which occupy some of your time—studying and going to class (the reason you are here in the first place!), sleeping, eating, getting ready every morning, etc. But when you subtract the average time needed for these activities, most students still have about 40-50 hours a week left. What options do you have to spend these "free hours"?

Some of this extra time may be spent working on or off campus or participating in intercollegiate athletics. However, it's important for you to explore opportunities in student life and campus activities, because there are many more benefits to being involved than just having fun (though that is certainly a benefit too!). Research over the past thirty years has shown that students who get involved in campus activities are more likely to have higher grades, more likely to

graduate from college, and more likely to develop a greater satisfaction towards their overall college experience than those students who choose not to participate in extracurricular activities. Also, being involved allows you to connect with students who have similar interests, pursue career interests and develop your leadership skills.

How do you find out what Berry has to offer in terms of campus activities? A great place to start is with the Student Activities Office, located off the Krannert Lobby. The staff can usually help you with your questions about upcoming activities or student organizations. Other opportunities to find out what's going on and/or to get involved in campus include . . .

- Attend the Student Involvement Fair which takes place early in the semester to find out about the various groups on campus and what activities they have planned for the year

- Participate in a KCAB event—there are over 40 events each semester, with the majority taking place on the weekends. These include talent shows, outdoor movies, comedians, trips, dances and much more. And what's even better is that KCAB events are usually inexpensive or free!

- Support the 12 Berry Athletic teams and cheer the Vikings on to victory

- Join any one of our 80+ student organizations (a complete list is available on the Student Activities website)

- Spend some time helping others by participating in a community service project–the Bonner Center for Community Service is a great resource for one-time or on-going projects

- Recruit some friends to form an intramurals team and compete for the coveted championship t-shirt

- Get involved in the Student Government Association as a hall or club rep or maybe even run for freshman class officer–SGA is a great outlet for finding out the latest events or issues on campus, as well as a place to have your voice heard

- Perform on stage, either through our theatre or music programs

- Explore your "journalistic side" and join one of our campus media groups

- Attend the many cultural events sponsored by various groups and academic departments

- Apply for Emerging Leaders, a freshman-only leadership program that encourages you to explore the various leadership positions at Berry and to develop your leadership skills

- Take time to read campus-wide emails, check out fliers, read the *Campus Carrier*, review KCAB's *Stall Wall Weekly*, or just visit the Berry website for the latest news and events

Now that you have the reasons to get involved and various resources to tell you how to get involved, there are a few words of caution to take into consideration. First of all, don't overdo it and commit to too many organizations or events. Learning time management is a key to a successful first year in college. Explore your options and commit to activities where you feel your involvement is meaningful but not too demanding of your time. Secondly, you don't want to experience "burnout" in your first year. Pace yourself. You have four years to take advantage of the many great activities. Third, don't do something just because "it will look good on your resume." Employers will ask you questions about your involvement and skills that you can transfer from college to the work world. Make sure that being involved is helping you grow and prepare you for life after Berry. You will find that it is all about the quality of your experiences, not quantity when you are interviewing for a potential job.

Don't miss out on the opportunities to be a part of campus life. As you can see, taking advantage of campus activities is a great way to enhance your overall college experience, while at the same time helping you find your "niche" at Berry. The best way to enjoy your college experience is to become an active participant in our community, so don't just sit there—GET INVOLVED!

My College Journey

Laura Sutton, Class of 2009 and SGA President

Change. Most of the time, that one word makes me cringe. I've always been the type of person that likes routine and structure. Change throws me off balance. But, if I could think of one word that sums up my college experience thus far, it would be change and it wouldn't be a bad thing.

Coming from a high school in Alabama to a college in Georgia was a big change. Sharing a room with not just one, but three complete strangers and having to wear flip-flops in the shower is not really something you can prepare for. For a while it was a tough transition. For the first time in my life I was really challenged to grow academically, spiritually, and mentally and to try on new roles.

I wasn't much of a leader in high school. I was a fairly shy, quiet student that kept to myself and worked hard. When I came to Berry I didn't have any intention of becoming a student leader. I had no idea what SGA was, but one night I found myself at a meeting. I became an SGA representative for a club my freshman year, and sophomore year I was the class secretary as well as a first-year mentor. These two experiences are the beginning of what I like to call "my college journey." During this year I began to see myself as a leader. I began to love serving with the goal of making a difference and leaving Berry a little better than I found it. I became more confident and comfortable in myself. I changed and matured. I was elected the SGA executive vice president for Campus Services in my junior year. It is hard for me to put into words how much I've learned from this experience. Working alongside faculty and staff has encouraged me to think critically and analytically in all situations. I've had many opportunities at Berry such as serving on the Provost Search Committee that will make lasting impressions on my life.

It's fun for me to look back at myself when I first came to Berry and to see how much I've changed . . . for the better. Now I can't even imagine being not being involved on campus. I love Berry and wholeheartedly believe in its mission of the head, heart, and hands. I hope that when I graduate I can continue to live my life with this mission in mind. I now have a love of learning along with a passion to lead and serve others. And even though change is still not my favorite word, my experiences at Berry have taught me to learn from it and make the best of it. So don't be afraid of change. Get out there and embrace it!

Money Management for Berry Students

Meredith Lewallen

Class of 2007

College really is the life. You set your own curfew, have access to your very own herd of deer, and have nearly 2000 people around to hang out with on a regular basis. You pick your own classes, decide which ones you will attend, and make some of the best memories of your life.

And, because Berry students are guaranteed on-campus employment, you also have something that many college freshmen don't: a steady paycheck. That biweekly check, however small it may be, means you can splurge a bit on luxuries like that bright pink comforter that matches your curtains or a $70 fancy dinner with that extremely attractive girl in your English 101 class. Necessary splurges like these are essential when it comes to living out the "college life."

Yes, you will spend a lot of money on useless things while you are in college, and yes those things are completely worth it. But just as you plan your days and weeks to make the most effective use of your time, you need to have a plan for your money, too. Following a few easy steps can guarantee that you will graduate in good financial condition.

1. Establish a Savings Habit.

   College is an ideal time to develop a savings habit. If you begin as a freshman saving $100 per month at 5% interest compounded monthly, you will have saved $226,428 by age 65. If you wait until your senior year to start saving the same amount, you'll have $191,613 by age 65. And if you wait until you're 25 years old to set that monthly sum aside, you'll end up with just $161,637 at 65. Now 65 seems like a long way off from 18 or 19, but the value of compounded interest can be applied to shorter term financial goals, such as paying off your college loans, making a deposit on your first apartment or buying a ring for that girl in your English class.

   It's easy to save money just by cutting out luxuries, but most college students have to pay for necessities such as gas, cell phones, food, and other expenses. Saving is not about putting away all of your money until you are broke. Saving is simply about putting money away *first*, even if it is just a small amount. The goal here is to figure out what percentage of your paycheck you can do without. Then, make sure that as soon as you get paid you put that money into a savings account. That way you will not be tempted to spend it, and it will be earning interest. And you can always save more or less money depending on your expenses at that particular time. Just make sure that you at least save something . . . even if it is only $10.00 a month.

2. Think Before You Spend.

   Another key to making it through college in good financial standing is to think before your swipe. Debit/credit cards make is so easy to pay for things without actually seeing the cash leave your hands. Make a conscious effort to think before you grab for your wallet. Do you actually *need* what you are about to buy? If the item is deodorant, then yes you do! But if it is a really cool blender that is on sale at Wal-Mart when you happen to be craving a smoothie in February, you might want to rethink your decision.

3. Pay Credit Card Bills in Full.

Credit cards can be a great convenience, but just making the minimum payment on your monthly bill can lead to big trouble. Let's say you go away with friends for fall break and run up $500 on your credit card and pay just the minimum payment of $10 when the bill comes due in November. If you continue to pay the minimum at the relatively low interest rate of 13%, it will take you 73 months (that's two years longer than college) to pay off the whole debt, and your $500 vacation will actually cost you $727.

So when you are thinking of having a nice big Outback steak, why not save that $20 and hit up Chik-Fil-A? Because you are bound to have a coupon for a free sandwich lying around somewhere, and that $20 bucks might one day turn into a new car!

Monthly Budget

MONTH_____

INCOME

Source   Amount

  1._____ $_____

  2._____ $_____

  3._____ $_____

  4._____ $_____

  5._____ $_____

              TOTAL: $_____

FIXED EXPENSES

Type   Amount

  1._____ $_____

  2._____ $_____

  3._____ $_____

  4._____ $_____

  5._____ $_____

  6._____ $_____

ANTICIPATED EXPENSES

  7._____ $_____

  8._____ $_____

  9._____ $_____

10._____ $_____

              TOTAL: $_____

TOTAL INCOME: $_____

TOTAL EXPENSES: $_____

Subtract expenses from income

BALANCE (Savings): $_____(Balance *must* be positive!)

Making a Major Decision

One of the first questions you may have been asked when you announced where you were going to college was, "What will your major be?" While some students have known since middle school what they'll be majoring in, others walk through the Gate of Opportunity without a clear idea of the major they want to pursue. And many of those students who enter with a major will end up changing it before they graduate. Choosing a major is one of the most important choices you'll make in college, so you shouldn't rush into a decision. Your major should reflect your strengths, values, and aspirations.

Don't Assume Choosing a Major Means Choosing a Career

What do Disney CEO Michael Eisner, Supreme Court Justice Clarence Thomas, and astronaut Sally Ride have in common? All three have undergraduate degrees in English. The conclusion to draw from this bit of trivia isn't that you should major in English if you have ambitions of someday presiding over a major entertainment conglomerate, sitting on the highest court in the land, or traveling in space. Rather, the point is that an undergraduate major isn't the surefire predictor of future career that many people think it is. It's true that some majors are better preparation for certain kinds of work than others; however, relatively few undergraduate majors lead directly to a specific career. Career goals should certainly be one consideration when choosing a major, but by no means the only one. And be advised that employers in any field will be as interested in what a potential applicant can do as in his or her college major.

Skills Matter

When thinking about a major, consider not only your interests but your skills and talents as well. How will the major help you capitalize on your natural talents and develop skills that may be weak? In a recent survey by the National Association of Colleges and Employers, employers ranked communications skills as the most important personal characteristic they seek in potential employees. Other important characteristics include strong work ethic, teamwork skills, initiative, and problem-solving, analytical, and flexibility/adaptive skills. Ask professors and upperclassmen how the major would help you develop specific skill sets. You should also inquire about internship opportunities for this major.

Think of a Major as an Intellectual Home

When you enter a major, you begin a concentrated course of study that will become increasingly focused and increasingly demanding. You'll be going to classes, working on projects, and probably socializing with other students as well as with professors in that discipline. It's important, therefore, that you enjoy not only the work but also the people with whom you'll be spending so much time. If you are drawn to a major because of genuine interest and curiosity about the subject, chances are you will feel at home with peers within the field; on the other hand, if you enter a major not out of real interest but because you think it will lead to a high-paying job, for example, or to fulfill parents' or teachers' expectations, you may feel out of place and uncomfortable.

A Good Choice is an Informed Choice

There are no quick answers to your search but there are many Berry College resources that are available to help you begin to sort, identify, and clarify what the right "major decision" is for you.

- **Berry professors and advisors** are always willing to share their expertise about their fields and the opportunities within the major. They will also have information on internships and career fields.

- **Fellow students** can give you the inside story on a major. Ask professors for names of juniors and seniors you might contact about their college major experiences.

- **The Majors Fair** held in September is a great place to talk with faculty in each discipline and find information on the various academic majors available at Berry College.

- **The Career Development Center** in Krannert Center holds a wealth of information about majors and career planning as well as tools and services to help students assess their own interests and abilities. Make an appointment to learn relationships between majors and careers, internship opportunities, and to obtain one-on-one assistance with college major and career decision making.

- **The college catalog** is a great resource for researching courses required for each major and for learning about specialized majors and tracks. You can access the catalog online: http://www.berry.edu/catalogs/0709/. More information and answers to frequently asked questions about each of Berry's majors and minors are available here: http://www.berry.edu/academics/majorlist.asp

Planning Forward and Looking Backward: Linking My Strengths and Talents to My Chosen Path and Interests

John R. Grout

Dean, Campbell School of Business, Berry College

What do you want to be when you grow up? I used to think this was a question you only asked little children. However, it turns out that I have continued to ask myself this question over and over during my adult life. Coming up with good answers to this important question isn't child's play either. As you progress through life, the set of possible answer becomes smaller. Being the dean of a business school is a great job; but, I have very limited ability to change career paths now. My age, qualifications, and a variety of other decisions severely restrict my choices. The good news is that I actually like what I have grown up to be and I am pleased with what I have accomplished. I continue to be interested in life and have aspirations and goals that make life interesting, engaging and meaningful. It is also important to recognize that I do have weaknesses that make some of my directions challenging and push me out of my comfort zone. In retrospect, what I grew up to be makes sense. Here is how my strengths and talents are linked to my chosen path and interests.

Looking Back

I remember making my mother angry occasionally, but I have never seen her angrier than when I brought home a 9th grade career assessment test. It indicated that my interests and aptitudes most closely matched a trade profession and recommended vocational training in high school. It reported that my chance of success in college was about 40%. Not a paying proposition. Smoke came out of my mother's ears and she started planning her attack on the school district hierarchy. Luckily for them, I pleaded and prevailed upon her not to go on the war path. But it was absolutely clear to me that I had better not give up on college yet.

In April 1984, I graduated from Brigham Young University with the top GPA in my major and having paid tuition for only three of the semesters I had attended. The remainder was covered by academic scholarships. A few years later, I returned to my hometown, where Penn State University is located, to pursue a Ph.D. A young friend invited my family to view a junior high school play in my old school. That night I had the opportunity to return to my old social studies room, the place where I was counseled against attending college. I enjoyed silently testifying to that place that the test was wrong, or at least that I had beaten the odds.

Most of the other interest and aptitude tests that I haven taken have turned out to be essentially correct. An early career interest test indicated that I should become a purchasing agent. At that time, I did not know what a purchasing agent was. Now that I know, I still think it does not sound like a fun job. I recently took the SIGI³ career interest test. My results generally match my earlier interest test. SIGI³ indicate that my interests tend toward engineering. My personality type is social. SIGI³ indicates that I value leisure and security most. Among my 18 preferred occupations are inventory control specialist, industrial engineer, and industrial purchaser (a.k.a. purchasing agent). Ironically, my Ph.D. dissertation is titled "Just-in-time purchasing: a game-theoretic perspective." My field of study, operations management, is closely related to the work of purchasing agents. It also involves inventory control and has significant overlap with industrial engineering.

In addition to StrengthsQuest and SIGI³, I've also taken the Meyer-Briggs Type Indicator, which identifies personality types. The results from StrengthsQuest and Meyers-Briggs correspond well with each other and to my own perceptions of my strengths and talents.

Myers Briggs indicates that I am "ISTP": introverted, sensing, thinking, and perceiving. Accordingly my comfort zone involves being an analytical "bookworm" type. Some may perceive that my external persona does not match this description. However for me, it matches well. Any outgoing-ness and social skills I have were obtained with difficulty through enduring uncomfortable circumstances. My field of study and work, operations management, fits well with ISTP. It benefits from analysis and does not generally require the behaviors of an extrovert.

My StrengthsQuest themes are includer, responsibility, belief, restorative, and connectedness. I currently fulfill several roles in my life. I am the dean of a business school, a teacher/scholar/mentor, a family man, and a church leader. My work as dean benefits from being an includer, from my willingness to bear responsibility, and from my strong set of core values and beliefs. As a scholar, I have written extensively in mistake-proofing, quality improvement, and process management. My approach to these topics is analytical, but unmistakably has restorative and connectedness aspects. A key principle at the foundation of all mistake-proofing is the existence and knowledge of cause and effect. Everything that can be controlled must have happened for a reason: the definition of connectedness. All of these topics are unquestionably focused on solving problems and improving things—clearly restorative. As a teacher and mentor my goal is to help students succeed and master difficult material. In fact, my distinctive ability in the class room lies in my ability to make difficult analytic material accessible to as many students as possible. I include as many students as possible within the group who understand the material. I also do my best to help students solve their problems with mastering the material and try to provide a supportive, encouraging learning environment. The strengths—includer, responsibility and belief—are pivotal in performing my roles as family man (father and husband) and as a church leader. A little problem solving seems to come in handy in both of these roles too.

My avocations are woodworking and woodcarving. The aptitude test that made my mother go ballistic was not all that far off. When I have the opportunity to spend free time, I spend it just as predicted in 9th grade.

My Plan

My role as church leader will be declining in the next few years. The church rotates leadership roles among congregation members every 5 to 8 years. My 5th year is completed in July 2008. When the change does occur, I will be called to some other role in the church. My youngest child is a sophomore so in three years, my role as family man will continue but its nature will change dramatically. I will be an "empty-nester." I plan to continue to teach, research and mentor students. Continuing to be dean will depend on my performance and success in achieving the objectives of the school and college. Since I am not ready to commit to being a dean for the remainder of my career, I will need to maintain a measured, highly leveraged research agenda. Currently I have two projects in the works. The first is the completion of a grant from the National Patient Safety Foundation with a doctor and his research technician at Columbia University finding risk mitigation strategies within a database of 30,000 medical near-misses. The other is an effort to apply the theory from my recent book on medical error prevention to the errors that occur in the related fields of architecture, engineering and construction (AEC). The result will be a jointly authored book with a University of California–Berkeley professor who is the director of the Project Production Systems Laboratory. Both of these projects seems to fit my circumstances well because they match my existing research stream and require only measured involvement of time and effort. This will leave me free to pursue the interests of the school and college as dean of the Campbell School. The leisure that SIGI[3] says that I value so much will have to come later.

Figure 1. Links between my personality, strengths, interests and talents and my chosen career path

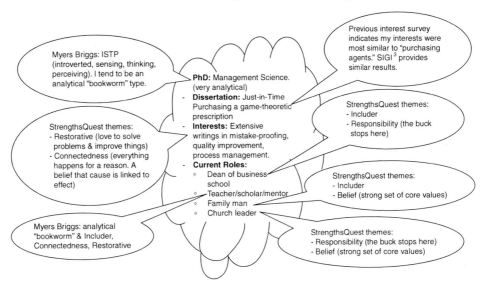

Healthy Habits for College Success

Maintaining good physical health is as critical to college success as managing time effectively and developing good study strategies. Not only will being in good physical shape keep you from getting sidelined by sickness and fatigue at critical work periods like midterm and final exams, but it will also help you to cope with the stress that accompanies such times. Furthermore, the habits you establish at key transition periods of your life (such as the start of college) often become permanent, so you may reap the rewards of a healthy lifestyle long after you graduate from Berry.

- **Eat a balanced diet of healthy foods.** Although nutritional needs vary somewhat from person to person, the US Department of Health and Human Services recommends a diet that emphasizes fruits, vegetables, whole grains and fat free or low-fat dairy products. They also recommend limiting the amount of animal and other fat in your diet by choosing lean meats and avoiding fried food, and including poultry, fish, beans, eggs and nuts in your protein choices. You can create a personalized nutrition plan and download some assessment tools online at http://www.mypyramid.gov/.

- **Eat regular meals.** Taking a full load of courses, working on campus and keeping up an active social life sometimes lead students to skip meals or eat on the run. While sleeping through breakfast now and then may not hurt you, a steady diet of junk food will. Berry's continuing dining service, open from 7:00 a.m. to 8:00 p.m. Monday through Friday, makes it easier to fit regular meals into your schedule. It's also a good idea to keep healthy snacks like nuts, granola bars and fruit in your room to give you a boost between meals.

- **Get enough sleep.** The same hectic schedule that can lead to poor eating habits can also cause students to cut corners on sleep. Many students skimp on sleep during the week, and try to catch up on the weekend, but irregular sleep can play havoc on both your health and your academic performance.

- **Exercise.** According to the Centers for Disease Control, moderate physical activity on a regular basis can significantly reduce most major health risks, yet almost half of Americans aged 14 to 21 are not active on a regular basis. If regular exercise was a part of your life before college, make sure that you continue that habit. If your high school routine didn't include exercise, now is an ideal time to start. Berry offers a variety of opportunities for physical activities to suit every interest and taste. The HPE department offers courses in everything from weightlifting to mountain biking to ballroom dance, and you will find a number of noncredit workshops and classes in areas such as yoga and belly dancing offered each semester. Taking advantage of Berry's popular and diverse intramural offerings will not only help you to stay fit but will give you a chance to form new friendships.

- **Pay attention to your emotional health.** Everyone experiences ups and downs, and heightened emotions are natural in the first few days of college. Prolonged stress and emotional problems, however, can interfere with your ability to perform well and get the most from your college experience. If you notice changes in your sleep habits (either inability to sleep or a desire to sleep all the time), a significant change in appetite, feelings of anxiety or anger or a loss of interest in activities that you used to enjoy, you may want to seek help.

- **Know where to get help.** The Ladd Center at Berry is staffed with professionals dedicated to helping you maintain good physical and mental health. At the Health and Wellness Center, a registered nurse is on duty every day and no appointment is necessary. Students can also make appointments to see a physician on campus two days a week. You can also visit the Self Treatment Center for common over-the-counter medicines. The Counseling Center provides free, confidential counseling to Berry students for a variety of personal issues including depression, anxiety, and interpersonal issues such as family and relationships.

It can be a challenge to stay healthy while taking a full load of courses, working on campus and keeping up an active social life, but establishing a routine now that includes regular exercise, a balanced diet and sufficient rest now will yield dividends for a long time to come.

Thinking about Drinking

Katherine Powell

Director, Office of First-Year Experience

On February 8, 2002, Daniel Reardon passed out after a night of drinking with his fraternity brothers at the University of Maryland. His friends put him to bed and checked on him throughout the night. In the early hours of the morning, they discovered that he was not breathing and called an ambulance. By the time he arrived at the hospital, Daniel was brain dead. It took a week before his parents could bring themselves to remove him from life support.

Unfortunately, Daniel's case is not an isolated incident. According to the National Institute on Alcohol Abuse and Alcoholism, "Each year, approximately 5,000 young people under the age of 21 die as a result of underage drinking; this includes about 1,900 deaths from motor vehicle crashes, 1,600 as a result of homicides, 300 from suicide, as well as hundreds from other injuries such as falls, burns, and drownings" (Alcohol Alert).

In addition, over 70,000 students a year are victims of date rape while under the influence of alcohol, and more than 600,000 students each year report being sexually assaulted by another student who's been drinking ("Binge Drinking").

Berry is a dry campus, but as many of you have already discovered, even Berry students drink, both on and off campus. Most freshmen are younger than the legal drinking age of twenty-one, but as you are no doubt aware, that fact doesn't deter some students from drinking either.

As an independent adult, you'll make your own choices about if, when, and how much to drink. As with any other decision, you'll want your choices regarding alcohol to be informed and thoughtful, not impulsive or pressure-driven. Here are a few facts to keep in mind.

1. **You don't have to drink to fit in.** There's a common misconception that all college students drink—a lot. It simply isn't true. The Harvard School of Public Health survey found that the number of college students who abstain from drinking is actually on the rise; 19 percent of students surveyed in 1998 said they didn't drink at all, up from 14 percent in 1994. And as the table on the next page indicates, Berry students are even less likely to drink than the typical college student.

2. **You aren't the only one your drinking affects.** Just as non-smokers can suffer from the effects of second-hand smoke, non-drinkers can suffer from being around someone who drinks irresponsibly. A loud drunk can keep the whole hall from sleeping or studying. A sick drunk who vomits all over the hall bathroom isn't going to win any friends either. And these are just the minor second-hand effects. Let's not forget the major effects like being the victim of drunk driving or alcohol-induced sexual assault, or spending the night in the Emergency Room with a roommate suffering the effects of alcohol poisoning.

3. **Alcohol can lead to unwise sexual choices.** According to "Facts On Tap," a web-site maintained by the Children of Alcoholics Foundation and the American Council for Drug Education, "As many as 70 percent of college

Percentage of Berry Students Who...

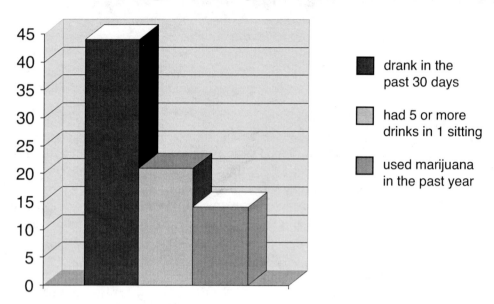

- ■ drank in the past 30 days
- ▨ had 5 or more drinks in 1 sitting
- ▩ used marijuana in the past year

Perception vs Reality: Percentage of Students Who...

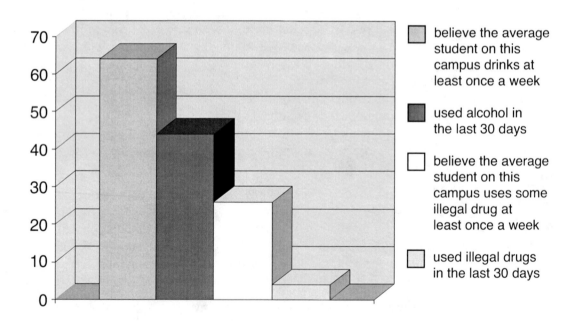

- ▨ believe the average student on this campus drinks at least once a week
- ■ used alcohol in the last 30 days
- □ believe the average student on this campus uses some illegal drug at least once a week
- □ used illegal drugs in the last 30 days

students admit to having engaged in sexual activity primarily as a result of being under the influence of alcohol, or to having sex they wouldn't have had if they had been sober." They also report that 20 percent of students say they generally do not follow safe sex precautions while drunk, even if they do so when sober. See Dr. Jenkins's essay on dating for more information on this topic.

4. Your parents may be notified if you violate Berry's drug or alcohol policies. Up until 1999, the college was prohibited from reporting such information under the Family Educational Rights and Privacy Act (FERPA), unless a student had signed an agreement to waive his or her rights under FERPA. Then,

Congress amended FERPA to allow colleges to notify the parents of any student under the age of 21 who was caught drinking or using illegal drugs, regardless of whether the student was a financial dependent of the parent. This also applies to those students guilty of joint-responsibility infractions pertaining to alcohol or drug violations.

Contrary to the prevailing cultural myth, excessive and irresponsible drinking is not essential to having a full college experience. In fact, recent research suggests that binge drinking for many students takes the place of more meaningful and productive activities. According to Dr. Henry Wechsler who directed Harvard's College Alcohol Study, "students who spend more time at such activities as community service, academic work, the arts, and political activism are less likely to engage in binge drinking." Your college years will pass quickly. How do you want to fill them?

Works Cited

Alcohol Alert Number 67. "Underage Drinking: Why Do Adolescents Drink, What Are the Risks, and How Can Underage Drinking Be Prevented?" U.S. Department of Health and Human Services. January 2006 **http://pubs.niaaa.nih.gov/publications/AA67/AA67.htm**

"Binge Drinking." Online Newshour. April 10, 2002. **http://www.pbs.org/newshour/bb/health/jan-june02/drinking_4-10.html**

Dating 101: Beyond Dinner and a Movie

Marshall Jenkins

Director of Counseling

Some people date in search of that one special person. Others date in order to get to know as many people of the opposite sex as they can. Still others date because they like to dance or laugh or be part of the action. Regardless of your reason for dating, there is one reason that everyone shares: to have fun.

If you are planning a fun date, the last place you will look for ideas is a college textbook. We all think of dating as something you just do without spoiling the fun with too many plans or rules. We expect dating to be as natural as walking or breathing or kissing.

In an important sense, that way of thinking is correct. After all, the best way to have fun on a date is to be yourself, and no textbook can tell you how to do that. But in another sense, that perspective misses an important truth: It takes a little discipline to have lots of fun. If we don't follow a few basic principles, dates become monotonous, frustrating, or downright dangerous. Here are a few guidelines to help you and your date be yourselves and have a good time.

Be Creative

People who ignore this principle get into ruts. Their dates consist of nothing but studying together or watching videos together or drinking together or having sex. Anything you do can feel like a trap if your dating life constantly revolves around a sole activity.

Young parents almost inevitably say that one of the greatest thrills of parenthood is seeing the world through a child's eyes again. It's the same with dating. Whether you and your partner spend one evening or the rest of your lives together, a date is an opportunity to enjoy life's many surprises and pleasures with someone else.

Communicate

There are two kinds of frustrating dates:

1. the strong, silent types who don't say enough for you to verify that they speak English and

2. the nervous chatterers who don't keep quiet long enough to draw a breath.

Fun dates balance talking and listening. Talking enables your date to find out more about you, although how you listen may help your date learn your most important qualities.

Communication not only adds to the intimacy of a date, but it also adds to the safety. Most date rapes involve miscommunication; for instance, she thought he wanted to relax together and talk on the couch, while he thought she wanted sex. Thus, it is important to discuss what you want to do on a date, where you are going, and what your values and limits are.

It may sound unromantic for the moment, but in the long run dates are much more fun and romantic if you discuss these things up front. Avoid mind games like assuming 'no' means 'yes.' Listen to your date's stated limits and respect them. If your date doesn't want sex and that's unacceptable to you, then you're in a rut, and you must go back to the first principle (be creative) to get yourself out.

Be Responsible With Alcohol and Drugs

Imagine that your date insists on driving but weaves back and forth across the center line, can't pronounce your name, interrupts everything you say with a knock-knock joke, gets angry or tearful for no apparent reason, threatens a passer-by with bodily harm, and throws up on the curb when you get home. Are you having fun yet?

Many drunks are not that bad. Some are worse. But one thing is for sure: That person is not on a date with you. That person is dating a bottle.

It is easy to be silly when you are drunk, but it is hard to be creative. It's easy to talk, but it's hard to listen. It's easy to be cool, but it's hard to be yourself.

Alcohol breaks down inhibitions, garbles communication, increases aggression in men, and diminishes physical strength in women. It takes fewer drinks to intoxicate a woman than a man. Little wonder that alcohol abuse is one of the top factors for date rape among college students. In 75 percent of all date rapes among college students in one survey, either the perpetrator or the victim was either intoxicated or "mildly buzzed."

Nobody wants to be a victim, and very few want to be a rapist. Everybody wants to have fun. In order to have fun without becoming a rapist or victim, know your limits with alcohol and respect the limits of your date. If you find your partner's limits frustrating, or you cannot imagine having fun without heavy drinking, you're in a rut. Refer to principle one (be creative). If that doesn't help, go to the Counseling Center. You need help getting out of this one.

Be Yourself

This was mentioned at the outset of this essay, but it bears repeating. Many people assume that dating is a game in which you guess what your date wants and then play that role. This maneuvering often involves silly stereotypes about what guys want or what women expect. True, it is important to be sensitive to your date's desires (although you certainly don't have to meet them). But if your date has enough maturity to be worth dating again, he or she mainly wants you to be yourself.

Being yourself is easier said than done. It helps to face your fears and deal with them. For instance, many people play a role that is not really them because they fear that they will bore their date if they share their true feelings, aspirations, and values. The best way to overcome that fear is to put it to the test: share your feelings with friends or dates. Chances are, you'll see that others find you interesting—especially if you show interest in them also. You don't need clever remarks or exotic experiences for people to find you interesting. The most popular person at the party is usually the one who speaks most genuinely and listens most attentively.

We are usually bored by people in ruts—people who are so caught up in themselves that they won't listen, people who can't have fun without getting trashed, people who hide behind a role because they haven't faced their fears, and so on. But with creativity; a balance of talking and listening; responsibility about alcohol, drugs and sex; and the courage to be yourself, your chances of getting into a rut are very slim. And your chances of having a good time on dates are very, very good.

Works Cited

Koss, M.P. and T.E. Dinero. "Discriminant analysis of risk factors in sexual victimization in a national sample of higher education students." *Journal of Consulting and Clinical Psychology*, 57, (1989): 242–250; and Koss, M.P., C.A. Gidyez, and N. Wisniewski. "The scope of rape: Incidence and prevalence of sexual aggression and victimization in a national sample of higher education students." *Journal of Consulting and Clinical Psychology*, 55, (1987): 162–170.

Abbey, A. "Acquaintance Rape and Alcohol Consumption on College Campuses: How Are They Linked?" *College Health*, 39, (1991): 165–168.

MY COLLEGE JOURNEY

Ellen Johnson, Associate Professor,
Dept. of English, Rhetoric, and Writing

I went to college at the end of the 1970s, the heyday of sex, drugs, rock and roll, and an 18-year-old drinking age. I had spent my high school years achieving perfection—on the outside at least—having a 4.0 GPA and being a leader in church youth programs and the darling of my mother's eye. On the inside, though, I somehow had the idea that if people really knew me they wouldn't think I was so great. Once I got 500 miles from home, I stopped living up to the high expectations of teachers and family, and started living up to my own low self-esteem. Having graduated from a not very rigorous public high school, my first blow was realizing that a majority of students at the prestigious liberal arts school I attended were also A students, and that many of them were A students at schools much more advanced than the one I'd attended. In other words, most people there were just as smart as me and mostly richer too. I think this is a problem for some Berry students who have been used to being the top kids in school, but find they are just average here. It may require an identity adjustment: finding out who you are beyond your school achievements.

It was easier to fit in and meet people when I'd been drinking, so this became a daily routine for me, along with taking whatever drugs were available at any given time. At some point, realizing I was drinking myself into blackouts most weekends, I went to the counseling center, but I was basically told that my behavior was typical for a college student and I would outgrow it. Don't fall into this trap of denial if you are telling yourself this! I had to go through some pretty painful experiences, but I was able to begin to recover from my addiction five years after graduating, and have continued to stay drug and alcohol free ever since. Looking back at the college experience, I do have some regrets. I do not have any lasting friendships from my college years. I now have a thirst for learning, and I think of the opportunities I missed to wrestle with great ideas. We all have our own paths to follow, however, and my struggle with substance abuse that began in college led me into a path of self-knowledge and spiritual growth that has brought me a peaceful and joyful life. I would encourage Berry students to get the help that's available to feel good about themselves and avoid destructive behaviors. Not everyone makes it out alive.

Academic Excellence

Remarks at Berry College Honors Convocation, April 2, 2003

Peter Lawler

Dana Professor of Government and International Studies

I'm supposed to say a few words about academic excellence.

So let me say first that I'm all for it.

And that I couldn't for the life of me define it, much less measure it.

Still, I'm sure there's a lot of academic excellence at Berry, because my experience is that Berry is almost a perfect place for it to flourish.

For one thing, academic excellence is often threatened by the restraints on academic freedom imposed by the doctrine of a particular religious denomination. Berry is connected with no religious denomination, which frees me to say good and bad things about various forms of faith as I think best in my classes. Academic excellence is also threatened by restraints on academic freedom imposed by government bureaucracies. Professors in state systems are constrained by fear of litigation, trendy and shallow political correctness, and unreasonably intrusive demands for accountability. But Berry is not a public school, and so our professors are not discouraged by meddlesome administrators and elected officials. Berry professors, I think, have much more freedom to teach what they think best than those at public colleges.

But there are lots of nondenominational private schools; what makes Berry unique is its three-fold purpose—the head, the heart and the hands. (I'm going to skip the hands, because a big reason I got into college teaching is that it involves no manual labor.)

So a word about the heart. By heart, Martha Berry meant religion. And her main way of cultivating the heart was making the students go to chapel regularly. Berry no longer does that, and chapel attendance is now small. But we do take religion in life seriously, and Berry has the reputation of having a religion-friendly environment. The result is we have a good number of very religious students. But because all religion at Berry is now voluntary and not directed by any particular religious denomination, we also have a good number of students who are only vaguely religious or not religious at all.

From one view, we don't have that much religious diversity at Berry. Almost all the students are Christians, although they do have very diverse views of Christianity. But from the point of view of intensity of religious belief, we have what seems to me to be a quite amazing diversity, and that diversity has genuine educational benefits.

When I was teaching a class on politics and the challenge of biotechnology the other night, I had to fight a two-front war: My own moderate and fair and balanced position was attacked by very smart, subtle, and intense theists and with equal intensity by anti-religious scientific relativists. One faction insisted that there is no human dignity without God, and the other that there is no such thing as human dignity at all. I wonder at how many colleges both of those factions would have felt so free to speak up. I wonder at how many colleges I would have felt perfectly free to fight back and even make fun of them both. Certainly each faction learned from the other, and I learned from them both.

Now I'm not saying that I don't find some of the religious intensity at Berry strange and irritating. As a Catholic, I'm puzzled when I hear of a mission trip to convert Poland to Christianity. And I'm going to resist giving my opinion of praise music and Veggie Tales. But maybe I'm just getting old. My only real point is that the genuine diversity of religious intensity of Berry saves lots of students and even our faculty from two great obstacles in the way of academic excellence today: a complacent and thoughtless religious faith and a vain or self-satisfied secularism. I'm happy to the extent that all the questions animated by the human experiences of faith and reason are really alive for our students.

Now a word about the head. By the head, Martha Berry meant the academic program, the classroom and lab. As far as I can tell, Berry's academic program has always been pretty secular. That's not to say that the heart has no place there; higher education should concern itself with all human experiences—including faith, morality, virtue, love, death, and God. Higher education should also involve reading the best books on the heart or love—like Plato's *Symposium*, the Bible, and Pascal's *Pensées*—with the thought that they really might be true. It's also true, of course, that professors who mess with students' heads also affect or even change their hearts.

But it's still the case that in the classroom everything is or ought to be disciplined by the head, by what human beings can know about reality through reason. When the discipline of reason breaks down in the classroom, teaching is replaced by therapy or fanaticism or therapeutic fanaticism. And even most of our very intensely religious students know and appreciate that.

A very devout and admirable but religiously very touchy student plopped down in my office a couple of years ago and almost screamed—"that class makes me vomit." It turns out that it was a class taught by one of our excellent religion professors. At the time, I have to admit that all I did was try to calm her down and ease her out of my office. But eventually it occurred to me that only a pretty powerful class could make a student vomit. And a class that moving, that engaging, other students might actually love. And the difference between loving and vomiting is not really so great, as anyone really in love will tell you.

More importantly, that sensitive student—who clearly thought her view of Christianity should prevail in the chapel—didn't challenge for a moment the right of her professor to make her sick. She even knew it wasn't good for her to expect the same treatment in the classroom as she might receive in a chapel or Sunday school. She understood well one aspect at least of the Berry distinction between the head and the heart.

The good news about academic excellence at Berry is that our students aren't bored or boring. They're readily and passionately moved to thought by the big issues that do or ought to make up every human life. They're not here just to take notes, pass tests, and eventually get jobs. And our professors are remarkably free to teach boldly what they think best, even when they seem unfashionable or even a bit offensive.

Overcoming the Culture of Silence on Race....

Beverly Daniel Tatum

President, Spelman College

"Raise your hand if you're ever had a difficult, distressing, ultimately unproductive discussion about race."

A roomful of hands usually shoots up when I've asked that question of students in my psychology of racism courses.

Even though we live in a nation where issues of race are continually in the news, few of us have learned how to talk across racial lines.

Our silence, aggravated by persistent social segregation, means that college is often the first opportunity many Americans have to live and work in a multiracial setting, and to engage in multiracial dialogue.

And I've seen how hard it can be and how frightened many people are to begin a conversation about race. But I've learned that dialogue about racism can be a powerful catalyst for change.

My students, both white and of color, readily admit their fears in their journals and essays. Some white students are afraid of their own ignorance, afraid that because of their limited experience with people of color, they'll ask a naive question or make an offensive remark.

While this sometimes does happen, silence is not without risk; students of color often interpret it as racist support for the status quo.

Because of the culture of silence about racism in many white communities, white students often haven't had practice at pushing past inhibitions to speak. They notice that students of color speak about racism more often and, they assume, more easily.

One white student observed: "In our class discussion, when white students were speaking, we sounded so naive and so 'young' about what we were discussing. It was almost like we were struggling for the words to explain ourselves. . . .

"It dawned on me that these students had dealt with this long before I ever thought about racism . . . .

[It's] almost like I was hearing about it for the first time. For these students, however, the feelings, attitudes, and terminology came so easily."

She's correct that most of the students of color in that classroom are more fluent in the discourse of racism and more aware of its personal impact on their lives than perhaps she had been. But she is wrong that their participation is easy for them.

An Asian-American woman in my class wrote about the difficulty of speaking: "I understand that some [white people] are trying, but sometimes they need to take bigger steps and more risks.

"I am always taking risks when I share my experiences of racism. However, the dominant culture expects it of me. They think I like talking about how my parents are laughed at, or how my older sister is treated on welfare. Even though I am embarrassed and sometimes get too emotional about those issues, I talk about them because I want to be honest about how I feel."

Who will tell her story if she doesn't?

An African-American student wrote: "One thing that I struggle with. . . when it comes to discussions about race is . . . .that I tend to give up when I start to think, 'She or he will never understand me. What is the point? Then I have practically defeated myself."

The anger and frustration of people of color is hard for some white people to tolerate.

One white woman in my class told me: "Often I feel that because I am white, my feelings are disregarded or looked down on in racial dialogues. . . . I also realize that it is these feelings that make me want to withdraw from the fight against racism altogether. However, I acknowledge the need for white students to listen to minority students when they express anger against the system that has failed them without taking this communication as a personal attack."

This is what one young student of color hopes for. She isn't seeking sympathy but dialogue partners who are wiling to listen when the conversation gets hard.

We can all benefit from what my students are learning. For meaningful dialogue, fear must give way to risk and trust. Different life experiences will lead to differing, often conflicting, perceptions of reality. But when people make the commitment to remain engaged, shared understanding and a collective vision for the possibility of social change can be achieved.

It's worth the effort. As a society, we pay a price for our silence. Unchallenged personal, cultural, and institutional racism results in the loss of human potential, lowered productivity, and a rising tide of fear and violence.

As students go off to college, let's hope they pack a little courage, and they find others equally brave to help them engage in the dialogue we need to make a difference.

Re-reading Question:

1. According to Tatum, discussing race issues is difficult for both white students and students of color. What makes it difficult for each group? What do students risk when they speak about race? What do they risk when they keep silent on matters of race?

Discussion Questions:

1. Tatum begins her essay with a question she asks of her students: "Raise your hand if you have ever had a distressing, ultimately unproductive discussion about race." How would you respond to that question? If you have had such a discussion, what do you think made it distressing and ultimately unproductive? Tatum cites several factors that she thinks contribute to our awkwardness in speaking about race. Can you think of others? Have you had a productive and meaningful discussion of racial differences or other differences, either in or out of the classroom? If so, what factors do you think contributed to making that discussion productive?

2. Tatum believes that it is important for college students to move beyond their inhibitions and discuss racial issues openly. Why? Do you agree? What opportunities have you had since coming to Berry to engage in formal or informal discussions of race or other cultural differences? What do you think the college could do to encourage meaningful dialogue about these issues?

Discovery Questions:

1. Tatum's essay focuses on race, but there are other cultural and physical differences that can lead to misunderstandings among people. Complete this statement in as many ways as you can think of: "I am _____." Try to think of as many descriptors as you can. Include physical characteristics as well as groups to which you belong. Now review your list. To your knowledge, have you ever been discriminated against or privileged because of your affiliation with a particular group or because of a particular physical attribute? What assumptions might people make about you on the basis of any of these factors?

    I am:

Keeping Faith

Flannery O'Connor

Author

Flannery O'Connor (1925–1964), a graduate of Georgia State College for Women and the prestigious Writers Workshop of the University of Iowa, was just beginning her career as a writer when, at the age of 25, she was diagnosed with lupus and returned to Milledgeville, Georgia, to live with her mother. Before her death at the age of 39, O'Connor published two novels and two collections of short stories that have secured her place as one of America's greatest literary talents. A devout Catholic, O'Connor explores the mystery of salvation in stories that are  *notable for their violence and grotesque humor. Despite her debilitating illness, O'Connor was a frequent lecturer. Alfred Corn was a freshman at Emory University in 1962 and was inspired to write to O'Connor after she visited his college English class. In his letter, Corn worried that his college education was causing him to lose his faith. O'Connor replied in the following letter.*

To Alfred Corn,   30 May 62

I think that this experience you are having of losing your faith, or as you think, of having lost it, is an experience that in the long run belongs to faith; or at least it can belong to faith if faith is still valuable to you, and it must be or you would not have written me about this.

I don't know how the kind of faith required of a Christian living in the twentieth century can be at all if it is not grounded on this experience that you are having right now of unbelief. This may be the case always and not just in the 20th century. Peter said, "Lord, I believe. Help my unbelief." It is the most natural and most human and most agonizing prayer in the gospels, and I think it is the foundation prayer of faith.

As a freshman in college you are bombarded with new ideas, or rather pieces of ideas, new frames of reference, an activation of the intellectual life which is only beginning, but which is already running ahead of your lived experience. After a year of this, you think you cannot believe. You are just beginning to realize how difficult it is to have faith and the measure of a commitment to it, but you are too young to decide you don't have faith just because you feel you can't believe. About the only way we know whether we believe or not is by what we do, and I think from your letter that you will not take the path of least resistance in this matter and simply decide that you have lost your faith and that there is nothing you can do about it.

One result of the stimulation of your intellectual life that takes place in college is usually a shrinking of the imaginative life. This sounds like a paradox, but I have often found it to be true. Students get so bound up with difficulties such as reconciling the clashing of so many faiths such as Buddhism, Mohammedanism, etc., that they cease to look for God in other ways. Bridges once wrote Gerard Manley Hopkins and asked him to tell him how he, Bridges, could believe. He must have expected from Hopkins a long philosophical answer. Hopkins wrote back, "Give alms." He was trying to say to Bridges that God is to be experienced in Charity (in the sense of love for the divine image in human beings). Don't get so entangled with intellectual difficulties that you fail to look for God in this way.

The intellectual difficulties have to be met, however, and you will be meeting them for the rest of your life. When you get a reasonable hold on one, another will come to take its place. At one time, the clash of different world religions was a difficulty for me. Where you have absolute solutions, however, you have no need of faith. Faith is what you have in the absence of knowledge. The reason this clash doesn't bother me any longer is because I have got, over the years, a sense of the immense sweep of creation, of the evolutionary process in everything, of how incomprehensible God must necessarily be to be the God of heaven and earth. You can't fit the Almighty into your intellectual categories. I might suggest that you look into some of the works of Pierre Teilhard de Chardin (*The Phenomenon of Man* et al.). He was a paleontologist—helped to discover Peking man—and also a man of God. I don't suggest you go to him for answers but for different questions, for that stretching of the imagination that you need to make you a sceptic (sic) in the face of much that you are learning, much of which is new and shocking but which when boiled down becomes less so and takes its place in the general scheme of things. What kept me a sceptic (sic) in college was precisely my Christian faith. It always said: wait, don't bite on this, get a wider picture, continue to read.

If you want your faith, you have to work for it. It is a gift, but for very few is it a gift without any demand for equal time devoted to its cultivation. For every book you read that is anti-Christian, make it your business to read one that presents the other side of the picture; if one isn't satisfactory read others. Don't think that you have to abandon reason to be a Christian. A book that might help you is *The Unity of Philosophical Experience* by Etienne Gilson. Another is Newman's *The Grammar of Assent*. To find out about faith, you have to go to the people who have it and you have to go to the most intelligent ones if you are going to stand up intellectually to agnostics and the general run of pagans that you are going to find in the majority of people around you. Much of the criticism of belief that you find today comes from people who are judging it from the standpoint of another and narrower discipline. The Biblical criticism of the nineteenth century, for instance, was the product of historical disciplines. It has been entirely revamped in the twentieth century by applying broader criteria to it, and those people who lost their faith in the nineteenth century because of it, could better have hung on in blind trust.

Even in the life of a Christian, faith rises and falls like the tides of an invisible sea. It's there, even when he can't see it or feel it, if he wants it to be there. You realize, I think, that it is more valuable, more mysterious, altogether more immense than anything you can learn or decide upon in college. Learn what you can, but cultivate Christian scepticism. It will keep you free—not free to do anything you please, but free to be formed by something larger than your own intellect or the intellects of those around you.

I don't know if this is the kind of answer that can help you, but any time you care to write me, I can try to do better.

Activities Freshmen Engaged in During the Past Year

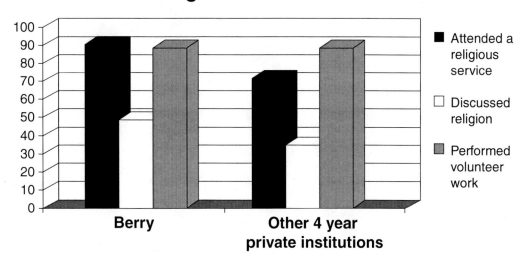

Re-reading Questions

1. In the first paragraph, O'Connor claims that the experience of losing one's faith "is an experience that in the long run belongs to faith." What do you think she means by this?

2. O'Connor seems to think Alfred Corn's worry that he will lose his faith at college is a concern common to many college students. What is it about college, according to O'Connor, that leads to this concern and discomfort?

Discussion Questions

1. O'Connor advises Alfred Corn, "If you want your faith, you have to work for it." In the next sentence, however, she says that faith is a gift. How can both statements be true? What do you think O'Connor means by "work for it"? What kind of work does faith require?

2. Discuss the following cases with your classmates. What advice would you give to the student in each case? What advice do you think O'Connor would give?

   A. Tom is enrolled in an introductory biology class. A significant portion of the course is devoted to the study and application of the theory of evolution. Tom rejects the concept of evolution on religious grounds and is therefore very uncomfortable in the class. He is thinking about dropping the course and looking for another science course to fulfill his general education requirement.

B. Lana, who thinks of herself as a political liberal, is a political science major. After taking Introduction to Political Science and attending several gatherings of the Political Science Club, she has come to feel that the department is dominated by political conservatives. She is thinking of transferring to another school where, she hopes, the students and professors will tend to think as she does.

Discovery Question

1. To what extent has your college education so far challenged your beliefs? Write a brief journal entry about specific ideas you've encountered in or out of class that have been inconsistent with your beliefs. How have you dealt with those challenging new ideas?

Claiming an Education

Adrienne Rich

Poet

Adrienne Rich is one of America's most distinguished poets. In her career of more than forty years she has received numerous prizes such as the National Book Award and the Poet's Prize. Rich has never been content, however, to simply receive praise for her poetry. Rather, she has spoken out in both poetry and prose to challenge traditional views of women and culture. In this 1970 convocation speech to students at Douglass College, Rich urges women students to take responsibility for their own education. As you read

this piece, consider to what extent her remarks apply to all students, not just women students. How useful is her advice to students today?

For this convocation, I planned to separate my remarks into two parts: some thoughts about you, the women students here, and some thoughts about us who teach in a women's college. But ultimately, those two parts are indivisible. If university education means anything beyond the processing of human beings into expected roles, through credit hours, tests, and grades (and I believe that in a women's college especially it might mean much more), it implies an ethical and intellectual contract between teacher and student. This contract must remain intuitive, dynamic, unwritten; but we must turn to it again and again if learning is to be reclaimed from the depersonalizing and cheapening pressures of the present day academic scene.

The first thing I want to say to you who are students, is that you cannot afford to think of being here to receive an education; you will do much better to think of yourselves as being here to claim one. One of the dictionary definitions of the verb *to claim* is: "To take as the rightful owner; to assert in the face of possible contradiction." To *receive* is: "To come into possession of; to act as receptacle or container for; to accept as authoritative or true." The difference is that between acting and being acted-upon, and for women it can literally mean the difference between life and death.

One of the devastating weaknesses of university learning, of the store of knowledge and opinion that has been handed down through academic training, has been its almost total erasure of women's experience and thought from the curriculum, and its exclusion of women as members of the academic community. Today, with increasing numbers of women students in nearly every branch of higher learning, we still see very few women in the upper levels of faculty and administration in most institutions. Douglass College itself is a women's college in a university administered overwhelmingly by men, who in turn are answerable to the state legislature, again composed predominantly of men. But the most significant fact for you is that what you learn here, the very texts you read, the lectures you hear, the way your studies are divided into categories and fragmented one from the other—all this reflects, to a very large degree, neither objective reality, nor an accurate picture of the past, nor a group of rigorously tested observations about human behavior. What you can learn here (and I mean not only at Douglass but any college in any university) is how men have perceived and organized their experience, their history, their ideas of social relationships, good and evil, sickness and health, etc. When you read or hear about "great issues," "major texts," "the mainstream of Western thought," you are hearing about what men, above all, white men, in their male subjectivity, have decided is important.

Black and other minority peoples have for some time recognized that their racial and ethnic experience was not accounted for in the studies broadly labeled human, and that even the sciences can be racist. For many reasons, it has been more difficult for women to comprehend our exclusion and to realize that even the sciences can be sexist. For one thing, it is only within the last hundred years that higher education has grudgingly been opened up to women at all, even to white, middle-class women. And many of us have found ourselves poring eagerly over books with titles like: *The Descent of Man; Man and His Symbols; Irrational Man; The Phenomenon of Man; The Future of Man; Man and the Machine; From Man to Man; May Man Prevail?; Man, Science and Society;* or *One Dimensional Man*—books pretending to describe a "human" reality that does not include over one-half the human species.

Less than a decade ago, with the rebirth of a feminist movement in this country, women students and teachers in a number of universities began to demand and set up woman's studies courses—to claim a woman-directed education. And, despite the inevitable accusations of "unscholarly," "group therapy," "faddism," etc., despite backlash and budget cuts, women's studies are still growing, offering to more and more women a new intellectual grasp on their lives, a new understanding of our history, a fresh vision of the human experience, and also a critical basis for evaluating what they hear and read in other courses, and in the society at large.

But my talk is not really about women's studies, much as I believe in their scholarly, scientific, and human necessity. While I think that any Douglass student has everything to gain by investigating and enrolling in women's studies courses, I want to suggest that there is a more essential experience that you owe yourselves, one which courses in women's studies can greatly enrich, but which finally depends on you, in all your interactions with yourself and your world. This is the experience of taking responsibility toward yourselves. Our upbringing as women has so often told us that this should come second to our relationships and responsibilities to other people. We have been offered ethical models of the self-denying wife and mother, intellectual models of the brilliant but slapdash dilettante who never commits herself to anything the whole way, or the intelligent woman who denies her intelligence in order to seem more "feminine," or who sits in passive silence even when she disagrees inwardly with everything that is being said around her.

Responsibility to yourself means refusing to let others do your thinking, talking, and naming for you; it means learning to respect and use your own brain and instincts; hence, grappling with hard work. It means that you do not treat your body as a commodity with which to purchase superficial intimacy or economic security; for our bodies and minds are inseparable in this life, and when we allow our bodies to be treated as objects, our minds are in mortal danger. It means insisting that those whom you give your friendship and love are able to respect your mind. It means being able to say, with Charlotte Brontë's Jane Eyre: "I have an inward treasure born with me, which can keep me alive if all the extraneous delights should be withheld or offered only at a price I cannot afford to give."

Responsibility to yourself means that you don't fall for shallow and easy solutions—predigested books and ideas, weekend encounters guaranteed to change your life, taking "gut" courses instead of ones you know will challenge you, bluffing at school and life instead of doing solid work, marrying early as an escape from real decisions, getting pregnant as an evasion of already existing problems. It means that you refuse to sell your talents and aspirations short simply to avoid conflict and confrontation. And this, in turn, means resisting the forces in society which say that women should be nice, play safe, have low professional expectations, drown in love and forget about work, live through others, and stay in the places assigned to us. It means that we insist on a life of meaningful work, insist that work be as meaningful as love and friendship in our lives. It means, therefore, the courage to be "different"; not to be continuously available to others when we need time for ourselves and our work; to be able to demand of others—parents, friends, roommates, teachers, lovers, husbands, children—that they respect our sense of purpose and our integrity as persons. Women everywhere are finding the courage to do this, more and more, and we are finding that courage both in our study of women in the past who possessed it and in each other as we look to other women for comradeship, community, and challenge. The difference between a life lived actively, and a life of passive drifting and dispersal of energies, is an immense difference. Once we begin to feel committed to our lives and responsible to ourselves, we can never again be satisfied with the old passive way.

Now comes the second part of the contract. I believe that in a women's college you have the right to expect your faculty to take you seriously. The education of women has been a matter of fact debate for centuries, and old, negative attitudes about women's role, women's ability to think and take leadership, are still rife both in and outside the university. Many male professors (and I don't mean only at Douglass) still feel that teaching in a women's college is a second-rate career. Many tend to eroticize their women students—to treat them as sexual objects—instead of demanding the best of their minds. (At Yale a legal suit [*Alexander v. Yale*] has been brought against the university by a group of women students demanding a stated policy against sexual advances toward female students by male professors.) Many teachers, both men and women, trained in the male-centered tradition, are still handing the ideas and texts of that tradition onto students without teaching them to criticize its anti-woman attitudes, its omission of women as part of the species. Too often, all of us fail to teach the most important thing, which is that clear thinking, active discussion, and excellent writing are all necessary for intellectual freedom, and that these require hard work. Sometimes, perhaps in discouragement with a culture which is both anti-intellectual and antiwoman, we may resign ourselves to low expectations for our students before we have given them half a chance to become more thoughtful, expressive human beings. We need to take to heart the words of Elizabeth Barrett Browning, a poet, a thinking woman, and a feminist, who wrote in 1845 of her impatience with studies which cultivate a "passive recipiency" in the mind and asserted that "women want to be made to think actively: their apprehension is quicker than that of men, but their defect lies for the most part in the logical faculty and in the higher mental activities." Note that she implies a defect which can be remedied by intellectual training; not an inborn lack of ability.

I have said that the contract on the student's part involves that you demand to be taken seriously so that you can also go on taking yourself seriously. This means seeking out criticism, recognizing that the most affirming thing anyone can do for you is demand that you push yourself further, show you the range of what you can do. It means rejecting attitudes of "take-it-easy," "why-be-so-serious," "why-worry-you'll-probably-get-married-anyway." It means assuming your share of responsibility for what happens in the classroom because that affects the quality of your daily life here. It means that the student sees herself engaged with her teachers in an active, on-going struggle for a real education. But for her to do this, her teachers must be committed to the belief that women's minds and experience are intrinsically valuable and indispensable to any civilization worthy the name; that there is no more exhilarating and intellectually fertile place in the academic world today than a women's college—if both students and teachers in large enough numbers are trying to fulfill this contract. The contract is really a pledge of mutual seriousness about women, about language, ideas, methods, and values. It is our shared commitment toward a world in which the inborn potentialities of so many women's minds will no longer be wasted, raveled away, paralyzed, or denied.

QUICK TIP

Set Deadlines And Publicize Them

If you tell your roommate, RA, mother, significant other that you plan to finish a first draft of your history term paper a week before it's due, you automatically increase your chances of doing so. Knowing that people will ask you if you've met your goal will motivate you to meet it. *For more ideas about managing time wisely, see Reading 2.*

Re-reading Questions

1. Explain the distinction that Rich draws between receiving an education and claiming one. Why does she think the distinction is an important one?

2. Rich says that while African-Americans and other minorities have long recognized the exclusion of their experience from most fields of study, women have been more reluctant to comprehend and accept that they too have been excluded. Why?

3. Rich says a college education implies an intellectual and ethical contract between students and their teachers. What are the students' obligations under that contract, according to Rich? What obligations do teachers have?

Discussion Questions

1. Rich says that women must insist "on a life of meaningful work...that work be as meaningful as love and friendship in our lives." Think about the work you intend to do in your life. Do you agree with Rich that work should be as meaningful as love or friendship? What kind of meaningful work do you envision yourself doing? What steps will you take to ensure that the work you do is meaningful?

2. Rich's remarks are addressed to women students at a women's college in the 1970's. Which of her comments are still relevant for female students today? Which are relevant for both male and female students? Are any of her comments irrelevant for students today?

3. Rich says that the most important thing to teach students is that "clear thinking, active discussion, and excellent writing are all necessary for intellectual freedom, and that all of these require hard work." What do you think she means by "intellectual freedom"? Why are all three skills necessary? Why is it important to teach students that all require hard work?

4. Rich says that students have a responsibility to take themselves and their education seriously and to demand that others do the same. What kind of behavior does such responsibility involve, according to Rich? What have you done, in the time you've been at college, to take responsibility in the ways Rich suggests? Can you think of times when you have failed to act responsibly?

Discovery Question

1. Writing more than thirty years ago, Rich observed, "Today, with increasing numbers of women students in nearly every branch of higher learning, we still see very few women in the upper levels of faculty and administration." Do you think Rich's observation still holds true? Use your college catalog to determine the ratio of women to men holding the titles of full professor, department chair, dean, vice president, or president. What is the ratio of women to men on your school's board of trustees? Discuss your findings in your next class session. What do your findings suggest about your college's commitment to equality of opportunity? What implications do these facts have on the type of education you might receive?

MY
COLLEGE
JOURNEY

Victor Bissonnette, Associate Professor of Psychology

I was born in a small Michigan town. My mother graduated from a Detroit high school; my father left high school to work on the farm during the Great Depression. During middle school, I was a promising student who was always curious and taking things apart. However, in high school I spent my time in cars and trouble, and I was lucky to graduate. After two years, I realized that I was wasting my life, and two friends and I decided to move to Texas to begin a new life.

At 20, I enrolled in two courses at Tarrant County Junior College. During registration, I completed some standardized tests of academic aptitude, and I remember a lady explaining to me that I had scored so low in math that I would need remedial classes in that area. However, what I remember most about that hot August day in 1981 was walking back to my car with a receipt in my hand that was stamped "paid" in big letters. I stood there for a moment looking at the buildings, and I realized that I had just acquired a brand new identity, one that really meant something to me. With tears in my eyes, I said to myself, "I am a student now."

I was surprised and happy to get a B on my first college exam. I knew that I wasn't prepared for college, and I feared that I would fail. I worked really hard on my studies, all the while working full time as a salesman. My old car and a cheap typewriter both got a lot of miles put on them. Over that first year, I earned good grades in all of my classes, and I came to realize that if I worked hard enough, I could parlay my meager academic skill into real growth and success in college.

I transferred to the University of Texas at Arlington the next year. In my first semester there, a history teacher named John Kushma changed my life. Mr. Kushma did not emphasize the "who" and "what" of history—he focused on the "why." Every class was full of interesting questions that inspired me to think. I would get to class early so that I could get a good seat for his energetic lectures. From that point on, I no longer looked at my studies as important and difficult; I saw my studies as important and fun.

Another thing that happened that first semester at UTA was that I flunked out of my first algebra class; that lady at TCJC was right about my math ability. I remember wondering, "am I good enough to be here?" The next semester, I enrolled in that class again, and this time I devoted a lot of time to working problems in the math lab. Not only did I pass that class, I earned an A in it. This experience taught me one of life's most important lessons: if you strive to grow in your life, sometimes you will fail. The question is, "what are you going to do about it?" That semester I learned that the best answer is, "be brave, try harder."

The semesters passed by, each filled with unique challenges and accomplishments. I settled on a major in psychology (my third major) because it is filled with interesting questions that inspire us to seek answers. I came to believe in myself as a student, and in 1986 I became the first person in my family to graduate from college. Since I had no idea what I wanted to do after college, I decided not to leave—instead I went to graduate school.

One day in graduate school I was teaching probability theory in a statistics lab (me, teach statistics!), and I realized that it felt completely normal and good for me to teach and to help other students learn. That day is also when I began to realize who I really was, and what I was supposed to become: a teacher. On a rainy day in May of 1992, I stood center stage in front of my family and friends. A colorful hood was draped over my robe, and the Ph.D. degree was conferred onto me.

That ends my college journey, right? No, I am still very much a student. I learn and ponder fascinating questions, and then I do my best to teach and inspire my students. And that is what I wish for you: a wonderful lifelong journey of learning and growth. Be brave, try hard.

The Story of Martha Berry

From Sources Distributed by Oak Hill and the Martha Berry Museum

Martha Berry was born October 7, 1866, and nurtured at Oak Hill, her father's plantation home near Rome, Georgia. When they were not engaged in more active pursuits, she and her five sisters and two brothers were tutored by Miss Ida McCullough, who often held classes in their log-cabin playhouse. When all the children were grown, Martha, who alone chose not to marry, converted the cabin into her personal den and study. A gifted storyteller, she wanted to be a writer. Sitting in her cabin one Sunday afternoon at the turn of the century, Martha heard children's voices coming from the woods outside. And then through her window she saw three boys in ragged overalls. Opening the door, she invited them inside to have some apples.

The boys ate apples while Martha told them stories from the Bible—stories to which they listened in awe and wonder until she was silent. Noting their keen interest, Martha was distressed when she learned there was no school the boys could attend. Then and there she determined to do something about their obvious thirst for knowledge. In this simple fashion began Martha Berry's lifetime work as an educator of the young people of her region. From the start, she made as her aim the education not only of the head, but of the heart and hands as well.

When the next Sunday arrived, the first boys brought their brothers and sisters to the little cabin, and soon their parents and other relatives began to appear. The Sunday School outgrew the cabin schoolhouse, and Martha moved her pupils to an old church at nearby Possum Trot, center of a small mountain community. As the group continued to grow, she opened other Sunday schools at Mount Alto and Foster's Bend.

Although she was delighted with the good-heartedness of the people who came to her Sunday classes, Martha was distressed by their woeful lack of learning. At the time she could not endure the thought that many bright boys and girls would never have the opportunity for real education. So to give them some chance, Martha decided to conduct day classes at each of the Sunday Schools. There were no free rural schools in the area. In fact, there were only five public high schools in Georgia. In 1901, with $1,000 of the money her father had left her, she built a whitewashed schoolhouse across the road (now U.S. 27, Martha Berry Highway) from her home, persuading the men and boys in her Sunday schools to do most of the carpentry.

But the day classes were not fully satisfactory. The children too frequently were kept away for cotton and corn planting, for harvesting, or because it was raining or snowing. Many of the hill roads were passable only at the mercy of the weather.

After a year, in January of 1902, she built a dormitory and opened a boarding school for boys. Knowing the rural boys of that area could not afford high tuition, Martha declared that every student would work to help meet his or her expenses. This meant the school needed land for gardens and pastures, and so Martha acted in her characteristic fashion. She took a property deed to town and told her friend Judge Moses Wright that she wanted to deed to the school 83 acres of land she had inherited. The judge and other friends of the family tried to dissuade her. "Let someone else do it," they said. But Martha prevailed and gave the land and even convinced Judge Wright to become one of her trustees.

Boys began appearing at the school at all hours of the day and night. The Boys Industrial School, as the new school was called, offered a high-school diploma. In those days a high-school education was less common than a college education is today. For many young men, the new school represented their only opportunity for secondary education. Appropriately, Martha named the entrance to her school the "Gate of Opportunity."

By 1909, Martha Berry had added a girls' school and Berry was rapidly becoming one of the nation's most successful educational experiments, combining academic study, student work, and interdenominational Christian religious emphasis. With an excellent record of sound growth, Berry established a junior college (1926), a four-year college (1930), and a graduate program (1972). Now one of the stronger colleges in the South, Berry is a model for many institutions in this nation and abroad. It owes its strength to the vision of its founder.

When Miss Berry died on February 27, 1942, thousands of friends across the nation mourned her passing. The *New York Herald Tribune* noted that she had died "full of years and full of honors." An editor of the *San Francisco Examiner* called her "a true patriot who gave her life for her country." The *Miami Herald* commented, "It is harder to live for one's country than to die for it, and America so needs a few more patriots like Martha Berry to stand by it."

QUICK TIP

Review Returned Tests

Whether you aced the exam of bombed it, take time to review it when you get it back. Check to be sure it's been scored accurately; professors do occasionally make mistakes. Note the questions that you answered incorrectly and try to determine the cause of your mistakes so you don't repeat them on the next exam. Look for patterns among the questions you missed. Ask yourself how you might have studied differently to do better. If you have questions about the professor's expectations or if you are still unclear about some of the material tested, make an appointment right away to review the exam with your professor. *For more on test taking, see Reading 9.*

Work, Learn and Serve: A Berry Tradition

Mike Burnes

Dean, Student Work and Experiential Learning

Berry College believes in the importance of instilling respect for worthwhile work well done. The Work Education Program has been an integral part of Berry's "Head, Heart, and Hands" mission since 1902 when Martha Berry opened the Boys Industrial School. As the school evolved into a modern college, the program has changed, but the principle of instilling in students the value of work and service remains.

At Berry, student work is more than just assigning students simple tasks in exchange for pay. Our program provides a unique opportunity to develop work skills, reinforce classroom learning, and contribute to the operation of the campus—all while earning wages to help offset the cost of attending college. The Work Education Program has three objectives:

1. Prepare students to enter the workforce by teaching work and leadership skills.

2. Provide experiential learning opportunities related to a student's academic studies and interests.

3. Ensure the successful operation of campus facilities and services.

Many Berry graduates recall their on-campus work assignments as the most memorable and rewarding of their college experiences. They often credit their success in the workplace to the values and skills learned from their campus work supervisors. Unlike most colleges and universities, Berry College depends on its student work force to operate the campus and provide essential services. Although participation in the Work Opportunity Program is voluntary, approximately 1,300 students choose to work on-campus each semester. As a result, student workers outnumber regular staff three-to-one. At Berry, your work makes a real contribution to your college's success.

Reflection on Work

Your work experience can impact your life in a number of areas. Answer the following questions in response to your campus work experience. If you are not working on campus, use the questions to reflect about past work experiences.

1. Personal growth: What has your work experience taught you about yourself?

2. Academic: How can your current work experience enhance your education? What future work opportunities might help you to use or build on skills or knowledge gained in the classroom?

3. Service to the college: How does your work contribute to the operation of the college?

4. Job and career skills: What skills have you learned or enhanced through your work experience? How might those skills be transferable to any future job?

5. Service to others: How have you served other students, faculty, staff and the community through your work? What has your work taught you about your responsibilities as a citizen in the Berry community and beyond?

6. Financial: How has the work program helped you to meet your financial obligations? How has it helped you learn about finances and managing your money?

MY COLLEGE JOURNEY

Tammi King, Post Office Supervisor

I came to Berry as a student immediately from high school, and was assigned to work in the Post Office. My supervisor was a wonderful lady named Eleanor Robison. I loved my job, and I loved her. She taught me about postage rates and bulk mailings, but she also taught me much more. Not only did I learn how to do specific tasks, but I learned why bulk mailings were prepared a certain way and why a customs form is important. She took pride in her job and saw the post office as a way to serve the Berry community. She taught her student employees that same work ethic. I first learned of Berry's three-fold mission of education—the head, the hands and the heart—from Eleanor Robison. She had high expectations of her student employees and took a personal interest in each of us. She believed in me and not only gave me responsibility, but also held me accountable for my work. She was my teacher and mentor and remains my friend to this day.

Later, I returned to Berry in a staff position in the Business Office. My job allowed me to get to know many faculty, staff and retirees, but gave me little opportunity to interact with students. When I transferred to the Post Office and became a student work supervisor, I realized that I had been missing what working at Berry was really about. Working at Berry is about being a teacher in the workplace. My role as a student work supervisor is a very important part of my life. It is sometimes challenging, but always rewarding. It is a relationship of mutual respect. I have supervised some of the brightest and most talented students who ever attended Berry College. They work hard, and I am sometimes surprised by their loyalty and dedication. I think Martha Berry would be as proud of these students as I am. I hope I have succeeded in teaching skills that can be used in every day life. I hope the students who have worked for me will return as alumni and share their post office stories! I hope their Berry College work experience has been as good as mine.

UNIT 3

TOOLS FOR SURVIVAL

INTRODUCTION

I hounded my mother into buying me several items I did not need. I did, however, need the red school bag. It was made of a sturdy, tarplike fabric, fastened by two metal hooks of the sort I believed secured Pilgrim shoes. She also bought a Fat Boy writing tablet and a blue, cloth-covered three ring notebook upon which I immediately drew a picture of my true ideal of a school house and also misspelled my name, in indelible ink.
—Kaye Gibbons, "The First Grade, Jesus, and the Hollyberry Family"

The right equipment is essential to the success of any journey. As you prepared to come to college, no doubt, you spent considerable time and perhaps a good deal of money thinking about and collecting the materials you would need. College success requires more than a good stock of notebooks and pens, however. It demands more than a calculator and a laptop. Equally important as these accouterments are the skills and attitudes covered in this unit. Although you probably already have some experience with most of the skills discussed here, many will need to be adapted for the college setting.

Most entering Berry students are used to conducting library research, for example, but will need to learn how best to use the services and resources available through Memorial Library. Likewise, note-taking, test-taking, and reading textbooks are nothing new to the average student; however, with the increased workload of college, many students find they need to develop a more thorough and systematic approach to these tasks. You will find too that many skills, such as critical thinking, critical reading, and writing, are ones that you are continually perfecting.

Some of the necessary survival tools discussed in this chapter may require a fundamental shift in thinking rather than actually acquiring new skills. For example, after reading Dr. McConkey's essay, you may view your college professors quite differently than you viewed your high school teachers; that new perspective will, in turn, lead to a different kind of relationship with them.

In the past year I frequently . . .

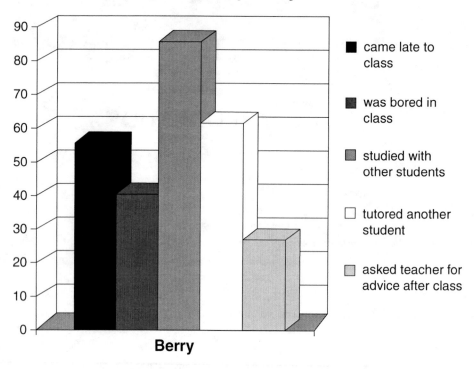

Berry

Legend:
- ■ came late to class
- ■ was bored in class
- ■ studied with other students
- □ tutored another student
- ▨ asked teacher for advice after class

So Much Information,
So Little Time . . .

Jeremy Worsham

Instructional and Digital Services Librarian

Martha Reynolds

Head of Public & Instructional Services

Information. It's everywhere. You're bombarded with it in ways that your parents never experienced. It's one reason you multi-task so efficiently! Now that you're in college, your coping mechanisms (for dealing with all this information) may need to change.

That perfect source: it could be available only as a podcast, or a dvd, or a book, or an original manuscript tucked away in some far away archive that requires a "road trip" like you've never experienced before, or a fleeting, controversial web site, or an eight-track tape (ask your grandparents), or a television news show transcript, or on a piece of microfilm, or as an article in some esoteric journal.

How to negotiate it all and still have time for the other parts of the "life of the mind" that you're about to experience? There is an answer: the library and the

people who work there (librarians) are all about connections, and guiding you from one source to another, regardless of what kind of container the information comes in! Your research travels here during the next four years will take you from print to media, media to web, web to original source, original source to secondary source, secondary source to primary source, in and out, to and from, over and over.

If you choose to limit your quest (for data, for information, for knowledge, for wisdom) to only those formats and tools for which you already have a high comfort level, such as the web or books, you'll miss out.

While you're at Berry, Memorial Library and the people who work here can help you do three things. First, we can serve as your trustworthy guide when it comes to information sources. Second, we can save you tremendous amounts of time if you will work with us. But the third and most important role we play is this: we can help you learn to develop and pose the right questions, whether for your personal research needs or for your academic coursework.

Memorial Library: A Place to Help You Stay Centered

- Bookshelves full of conflicting ideas and viewpoints
- Major online resources comparable to those of a large university
- Coffee or a Smoothie
- Expertise (librarians and professors who hang out in the library)
- The perfect anonymity and quiet solitude of an individual study carrel at the back of the building
- The imperfect, not-so-quiet, friendly and comforting buzz up front
- Laptops that circulate
- Scanner and fax machine for student use
- A sophisticated DVD collection
- A place of great tradition
- A place of constant change

Information Literacy Quiz

In preparation for the library orientation workshop you'll attend, try your hand at the questions below. They're "thought" questions where understanding the significance of the question is more important than knowing the exact answer. Be sure to bring this quiz with you to your library workshop session.

1. What makes someone "information literate"?
   A. the ability to read complex documents
   B. The ability to locate, evaluate and use information effectively
   C. the ability to search the "free web" for information
   D. the ability to summarize information you read

2. In 2002, the amount of new information produced in print, film, magnetic and optical storage media (not including the World Wide Web) was equal to
   A. A pickup truck filled with books
   B. All printed materials in one Academic Library
   C. 500 thousand libraries with collections the size of the Library of Congress (19 million books and other print collections)

3. According to an IDC study, in 2006 how many gigabytes of digital information existed on computers and digital devices worldwide?
   A. One hundred
   B. One thousand
   C. One million
   D. 161 billion

4. The worldwide digital universe is equal to approximately 3 million times the information in all the books ever written. If you were to stack books from here to the Sun, how many stacks would it take to equal this amount?
   A. 1
   B. 3
   C. 6
   D. 12

5. On average, how many visits per year do Memorial Library's web pages receive from students and faculty at Berry?
   A. 8,000 – 10,000
   B. 10,000 – 75,000
   C. 75,000 – 100,000
   D. 100,000 – 150,000

6. If you type in "socialism and Canada" as your keyword search phrase in a database such as Academic Search Premier, your search results list will include
   A. All records that include both the words 'socialism' and 'Canada'
   B. Any record that includes either the word 'socialism' or the word 'Canada'
   C. Only records that have 'Socialism and Canada' as the title of the journal
   D. Only records that have 'Socialism and Canada' as the title of the article

7. A bibliography is a list of:

    A. Information Sources

    B. Geographic sites

    C. Libraries

8. At Berry, your instructors will require you to use articles from "scholarly" rather than "popular" journals. Which of the following are characteristics of "scholarly" journals? (Select all that apply.)

    A. Articles are written for the general public

    B. Lots of glossy, appealing photographs

    C. Issues have few, if any advertisements

    D. Articles focus on coverage of current events

    E. Articles are written by experts in the field and have been evaluated by other experts prior to publication

9. Students do not need to be concerned about copyright issues because educational uses of information are exempt from copyright rules.

    A. True

    B. False

10. Searching Google Scholar from on campus will show you the resources that are available here at Berry.

    A. True

    B. False

Bibliography

Frick, T. W. (2005). *What is plagiarism?* Retrieved 5/28/2008, from http://education.indiana.edu/~frick/plagiarism/item1.html

Frick, T. W. (1991). *Restructuring education through technology.* Bloomington, Ind. : Phi Delta Kappa Educational Foundation, c1991.

Taking Good Notes

Rebecca Phillips

Class of 2011

It's the day of your first exam, and you get to class a little early to look over your notes one more time before taking the test. Suddenly, Jane, the girl you sit next to bursts into the room, out of breath and obviously frazzled. "I am not ready for this test at all." She confesses. "I couldn't even make sense of my notes when I tried to study last night." Jane pulls out a spiral-bound notebook stuffed with tattered pages and lots of quickly scribbled notes, and it's clear this isn't her notebook just for this class, but for all of her classes. No wonder she doesn't feel prepared.

Taking notes is more than just an activity to fill class time. It is an essential survival skill. Your notes are the record of what was covered in each class, as well as the study materials you will have later on, so it is important to develop excellent note-taking habits from the start.

Discussion vs. Lecture

In college, there are two main categories of classes. In a discussion class, an instructor leads students in conversation as a means of discovering and gaining better understanding of the ideas or subjects at hand. For example, philosophy classes are often discussion-based, allowing students to reflect on the information and exchange ideas with each other, as well as the professor. Discussion classes are usually engaging, but students often neglect to take notes either because they are too caught up in the conversation to stop and record it, or because they have difficulty discerning the important ideas among the rapid give and take.

In a lecture class, the instructor presents the information and explains it in detail. Although students can ask questions and engage in a dialogue with the professor, a lecture class is very information-oriented and is focused on the professor's presentation. Lecture classes present different note-taking challenges. Students often find it more difficult to stay attentive when the professor does all the talking. It can also be a challenge to keep up with a complicated lecture and to quickly and accurately record all the essential points.

Getting Started

Although you will want to adapt your note-taking strategies to suit your own learning style and the demands of each class, these simple steps will help you take notes that you can really use.

1. **Keep notes separate for each class.** Remember Jane? Because she kept all her notes for every class in one notebook, she couldn't locate them when it came time to study. Don't overestimate your memory! Have a separate notebook for each class, or, if you must use one notebook, make sure that it is clearly divided into sections for each class.

2. **Date your notes and number the pages to keep them in order.** This will provide you with a reference to indicate a specific set of notes.

3. **Put the topic of the lecture or discussion at the top of the page.** Again, reviewing your notes later and recalling information is much easier if the information is grouped appropriately. Labeling your notes in this way will allow you to locate them quickly and easily.

4. **Re-copy your notes as soon as possible after class.** The act of re-writing the information will enhance your ability to recall it later. Copying your notes while the class is still fresh in your mind will allow you to fill in any missing or incomplete information or to make note of questions you want to bring to your professor. As you re-copy, you'll also organize your notes better, which will save you a step later when it comes time to pull your notes together to study.

How Do I Know What to Write Down?

Because there is so much information offered in class, it is nearly impossible to write everything down. As you become more used to the daily structure of your classes, you will be able to pick out the information you need to write. The following tips are some guidelines to help you know what to look for as you develop your note-taking skills.

The Professor

Whether in a lecture class or a discussion class, what the professor says is of the utmost importance. Even so, do not feel obligated to take down every word that comes out of his or her mouth. Professors will give you some clues to help you make the distinction:

- Write down key terms and their definitions

- Write down important questions that the professor poses

- Write down any information that the instructor signals with verbal cues, such as "The main point is . . ." or "The discussion will focus on . . ."

- Write down information that is repeated or emphasized
- Copy anything that the professor writes on the chalkboard or on the overhead projector

Classmates

In a discussion-based class, your classmates are just as much a source of insight and information as the professor. Be sure to write down any thought-provoking ideas your classmates offer.

Getting to the Point

Again, you should never write everything down; chances are you won't be successful if you try. The best way to get the maximum amount information is to focus on the main points. Don't worry about writing in complete sentences—use shorthand and abbreviations that you are familiar with so that you won't be confused when you review your notes. Group main points with their details as much as possible, leaving space in between each main point so that you know where one ends and another begins. Finally, underline, highlight, or star important material so that you do not have to waste time searching for it later.

Strategies

All the suggestions up to this point cover the basics of taking notes. Another helpful tool is to have a note-taking method that works for you. Here are some possibilities you may want to consider:

Outlining

Outlining is a very familiar method to most note-takers that uses numbers, letters, Roman numerals, and so on to group major and minor points. Should you choose this method, beware of the confusion it can cause if you have trouble distinguishing major points and details. Instead of trying to keep to a formal system, you might want to opt for an informal system, using your own bullet points, numbering, and lettering.

Two-Column System

Fold your paper in half to make two columns. In the left one, write down the topic or question being discussed. Whenever a new point is introduced, also write down a new question or phrase that reflects the topic. In the right-hand column, write down the important information that corresponds to the topic or questions.

Label-in-the Margin System

Begin by folding your paper so that you have two columns. In the left margin, write questions for key points. In the right column, write down your notes. Summarize the information at the bottom of the page.

**QUICK
TIP**

Listening: where it all begins

In order to get the most out of every class, you must practice "active listening," which is the foundation for taking good notes. This means that you must not settle for simply hearing the information, but you must seek to understand it by processing it and drawing connections.

How to be an "active listener":

- Look for something of interest.
- Focus on content rather than style.
- Listen for main ideas.
- Change your note-taking habits to fit the content.
- Work hard to maintain attention.
- Sit up straight and maintain an "active body posture."

MY COLLEGE JOURNEY

Jennifer Klappich

Although I was diagnosed with ADD in middle school, I never stayed on the medication that was prescribed for me. I felt that taking medication was a weakness, and I am not a weak person. I finished high school at the top of my high school class, with great grades, and tons involvement in community service, sports, and school organizations, which only confirmed my belief that I didn't need any help. I was confident that I would be able to get through college on my own, too.

You can imagine my surprise when I bombed my first semester here at Berry College. I went into my second semester with bad grades, lying to my parents, my friends, and myself. On the outside I was the calm, cool, collected girl I always was, but on the inside I was breaking down. I studied constantly, but never saw the effects of my hard work.

By the end of my freshman year I wasn't sleeping and I was having such severe panic attacks before class that I would make myself sick.

I went into summer vacation with a 1.7 GPA. Finally, I told my parents what was going on and that I wasn't going to go back to school. They were disappointed, but they were supportive of my decision to take a year off and work. But I wasn't. I knew that the only reason I wanted to take that year off was because I was to afraid to go back to school, face my mistakes and try to improve.

Over the summer I started seeing a therapist, who prescribed a low dose of anti-depressants. My therapist also suggested that I be tested for learning disabilities again. The tests confirmed that I have ADD and a mild form of dyslexia.

My parents and my medical/therapeutic support team helped me come to the decision that dropping out of school wasn't the best path for me. They convinced me that I needed to come back to Berry and face myself. The school was very understanding and when I explained my problems, they were quick to make accommodations to try and help me be a more successful student. First semester sophomore year was still a difficult one and I still wasn't doing as well as I would have liked. I was still unwilling to ask my professors for the accommodations that I was entitled to, such as extended testing time, and I still refused to take any medication for ADD. To do so, I thought, would be cheating; I would be getting more than the average student.

Over winter break my beloved Grandfather passed away. My grandfather fought in World War II and he suffered from untreated PTSD for the rest of his life, which made it hard for anyone to get very close to him. Reflecting on his life and death I realized how short life is and that you have to live to the fullest. I realized, through him, that you couldn't always live life in fear.

When school started, I met with my advisor. I wanted him to know what was going on and why my grades were the way they were. I admitted that I was afraid people would think I was making excuses. I knew that my bad grades were only due in part to things beyond my control; in the end it was my fault for not seeking help. I told my advisor all of these things, and more, in our meeting.

I learned that day why we have advisors. Not only did he advise me, he helped me understand that taking help and using the support systems that the school has set up isn't cheating. He said that school is like a sports game and often times students who are receiving extra help feel like they are going onto the field with better equipment than every other player, or that they may even have equipment that no one else does. However, he said that the truth was that students receiving extra help started the game without all of the equipment necessary to play and that the help that the school offers only equips them so they are on equal footing with other students.

It has taken me a long time, but I am finally learning what I have to do to be a successful college student and a successful person overall. If you are having trouble and you don't tell people what is going on they won't know (professors are smart, but they are not mind readers). But students need to know that the majority of professors at Berry College do care about their students and want them to be successful. They've known all along what I now know, that asking for and taking help shows that you have the strength to rise above yourself and admit that you are not a perfect person.

Reading in College

Rebecca Phillips

Class of 2011

Reading is a fundamental skill required for academic success. You've known that since elementary school, and presumably you've developed your reading skills throughout your career, or you wouldn't have reached this point. Nevertheless, the reading expectations in college may catch you by surprise.

One obvious difference may be the quantity of reading—it will likely be more than you're used to. But another important difference will be the type of reading material. In college, you will be exposed to a wider variety of reading materials, each of which you will have to approach differently.

Let me show you what I mean by giving you a tour of the required reading for a course I'm taking in my first year as an English major, ENG 240, Literary Theory.

Types of Reading Material

Textbooks

Textbooks will most likely be the main type of reading material for your introductory and core classes and perhaps even for your major. Textbooks provide a subject's core information in a straightforward manner with lists, bold words and headings, definitions, pictures, charts, summaries, etc. For example, my Literary Theory textbook, *Critical Theory Today* by Lois Tyson, offers thorough explanations of the different schools of criticism and defines key terms and ideas associated with each one.

Primary Sources

In addition to my textbook, I am required to read several other books for ENG 240, including *The Great Gatsby* by F. Scott Fitzgerald. I know this is not a textbook because I'm having way too much fun reading it. So how does it fit into the reading material for the class? Well, it is a classic example of a primary source.

Primary Sources are original documents or works that offer first-hand information and opinions on a subject, and they are typically independent of other works. The Great Gatsby is a work of fiction set in the 1920's. Trimalchio, Fitzgerald's original draft of the novel is another primary source that lends insight into Fitzgerald's writing process and his relationship with his editor, Max Perkins.

Secondary Sources

Secondary sources are supplemental material for primary sources. They offer new, original ideas and provide analysis, critiques, and explanations of particular subjects. Unlike the factual information textbooks give, secondary sources evaluate the subject matter by offering opinions and interpretations, which are typically the result of much research. There are various forms of secondary resources:

- Articles—These are short, independent pieces of non-fiction. For example, Kent Cartwright's article "Nick Carraway as an Unreliable Narrator" is an article that explores the reliability and role of the narrator, Nick, in *The Great Gatsby*.

- Books—These are lengthier and more detailed commentaries that discuss further ideas on currently existing subjects. One example is Ronald Berman's book entitled *The Great Gatsby and Modern Times*, which analyzes and interprets Fitzgerald's work.

- Academic Journals—These are published in every field of study and contain several articles by scholars. Journal articles present recent studies or new twists on old ideas, which are the results of extensive research. For example, Kent Cartwright's article can be found in an issue of *Papers on Language and Literature*, an academic journal that publishes articles and research in the field of literature.

So What's the Point?

As you will come to realize, reading in college takes on a crucial role because it is necessary for preparing for class, not only for supplementing it. Reading exposes you to basic information and ideas that the upcoming class will focus on. Professors will generally not cover the information from the reading but will build on it, requiring you to be familiar with the information in order to participate and follow along in class. If it is a discussion class, you will be asked to reflect on the reading and offer your own thoughts and opinions. If it is a lecture class, your professor will expound on the basic ideas and connect them to previous ones or to new material.

General Tips

The amount and variety of reading in college necessitate that you develop strategies to handle it. There is no one way to approach all types of reading, but the following tips can be a place to start. Remember, reading is most often a means of preparing for your next class lecture or discussion, so make the most of your assignments.

- Stay on schedule with your readings and complete them before class. Most professors will list your readings on the class syllabus.

- Take notes on what you're reading.

- Pay attention to headings: the bigger the heading, the more important the information.

- Write down page numbers to reference important information.

- Pay attention to main points and look up unfamiliar terms.

- Recite the important information out loud and quiz yourself.

- Write your own summaries, visual maps, flash cards, etc., to absorb all the information.

Reading Textbooks

In order to successfully draw and retain information from reading your textbooks, you need a strategy. The following suggestions are ways you can get the most out of your reading in an organized, efficient manner.

- Label in the Margin

    1. Survey the chapter—Familiarize yourself with what the chapter is about and pay attention to the title, introduction, and summaries. Surveying should only take a few minutes and should prepare you for a more thorough reading of the chapter.

    2. Focus—Eliminate distractions and use the information you gained from surveying the chapter to help you understand what the main points of the chapter are.

    3. Read—Go paragraph by paragraph, allowing yourself to pause after each one so that you can fully grasp the information.

    4. Label—In the margins or on a separate sheet of paper, write down any questions you may have.

    5. Answer—After you finish reading, go back and underline or highlight the answers to your questions, as well as any main points or key terms.

- SQ4R

    - Survey—Get an idea of what you will be reading about and what the main point(s) might be.

    - Question—If you come across a topic you don't understand while surveying or reading the chapter, write down any questions you might have about it.

    - Read paragraph by paragraph.

    - Record the information—Take notes on what you're reading. The act of writing down the information will help you remember the information longer.

    - Recite answers to questions, key terms and their definitions, etc.— Repeating information to yourself is another good way of making sure you retain it.

    - Review the information—Make sure you review as immediately as possible to make sure the information stays with you. Then review later on to prepare for class and tests.

Reading Primary and Secondary Sources

As you progress in your college career, you will devote much more time to reading various primary and secondary sources in addition to or in place of textbooks. To help you understand the information, there are some questions to consider as you read:

1. When was the book/article published and by whom?

    The date of publication will tell you how recent the information is. Also, familiarizing yourself with the author and his or her credentials will give you some background information and help you understand what approach the author might be taking. This information is useful for understanding any assumptions that the author may have about the subject at hand.

2. What main point is the author trying to communicate?

Primary and secondary sources always give opinions on a subject. You should always read with the purpose to uncover the author's position first.

3. Does the author effectively support his or her main points?

Details do have their place in primary and secondary sources. Once you understand the main points, consider how the author supports his or her argument. Pay attention not only to the general claims the author makes, but the evidence and analysis offered to support them. Well-supported arguments will follow the thesis, include accurate information, cite other reliable and appropriate sources, and come to a logical conclusion.

Preparing for Exams: Right from the Start

Any professor will tell you that exam preparation begins on the first day of class. As soon as you receive your course syllabi, you should note and record the date of each exam. The best way to make good grades on your exams and to eliminate test anxiety is to attend class faithfully, complete all reading and homework assignments, take good lecture and reading notes and review them on a regular basis, and seek help as soon as you need it—not after you've failed your first test.

Even if you've followed all these steps, however, you may still find yourself feeling anxious as you approach your first college tests. Sometimes students report having studied hard throughout the term and still performing poorly on exams—either because they were overcome by test anxiety or because the exams didn't cover what they had studied.

In *What Smart Students Know*, Adam Robinson, co-founder of the *Princeton Review*, encourages students to think of an exam as a performance—an opportunity to show what you know. Robinson says: "To rehearse for a performance, you must practice. Rehearsing for a test means practicing what you'll be doing on a test—recalling information, organizing it, and applying it to answers" (177). Obviously, knowing the kind of test you'll be facing is crucial to planning your preparation.

Before you start rehearsing for an exam, you need to answer the following questions:

- How much time is the test expected to take? A class period? A two-hour exam period?

- Which material will be covered on the test?

- What kinds of questions will be on the test? Multiple choice? Short answer? Essay?

- How many points will be given for each section of the test?

- Will you be allowed to refer to your notes or text(s) for any part of the test?

- What materials will be required/permitted? For example, will you need a blue examination booklet? Are you allowed to bring a calculator?

Your instructor will probably provide an overview of the exam during class, or he or she may provide that information in the syllabus. If you still have questions about the type and content of the exam, don't be afraid to ask.

Once you know what the test will cover, follow these steps:

1. Gather all of your notes, handouts, quizzes etc.

2. Sort and organize information in a way that will help you remember it. For example, if you need to remember a sequence of events and dates for a history test, it would be helpful to create a **timeline.** If you need to be able to show how a principle applies to various phenomena, a **table** or **matrix** would be useful ways to organize the information. If you need to restate or explain an argument or theory, creating an **outline** would help you to remember the main ideas and key supporting points.

3. If possible, get together with a **study group.** Studying with two to four other students in the class offers the following advantages:

   • It provides multiple perspectives on the material being studied. You can check your understanding and comprehension against others'. Comparing notes and materials lets you see if you've overlooked anything.

   • It provides motivation to complete tasks on time. If you've told your group that you'll have a study guide for chapter 6 prepared for the next meeting, chances are you'll follow through rather than let down the group.

   • It provides an opportunity to perform. You may be asked to explain a theory or work a problem for someone in the group who doesn't get it. That kind of demonstration of knowledge is what you'll be expected to do on the test.

Study groups are most effective when all members are equally committed and responsible. Assigning tasks to each member before you meet will make those meetings most productive. You might, for example, assign every member the task of writing five short answer questions for the others to answer or condensing a section of class notes.

4. Anticipate questions and try to answer them. If you know what kind of questions will be on the test, write your questions in those formats. Essay questions require you to think about "the big picture." It's not enough to simply know facts, you'll be required to show how information is connected, why it is relevant, or how it applies to a given situation or problem. Objective questions such as multiple choice, true-false, or matching, on the other hand, generally ask for recall of specific information. They require you to pay more attention to detail. To get an idea of the kinds of questions you may face on an exam, look at old tests or quizzes if they are available. Most textbooks also have some type of comprehension questions at the end of each chapter—use them.

5. Avoid cramming. Despite the stereotype of college students pulling all-nighters before the big exam, cramming is one of the least effective ways to prepare for an exam. The name says it all—you may be able to cram a lot of information into your short-term memory and keep it there long enough to spill it out onto a test, but you'll forget it as soon as the test is over.

6. Get all your materials ready in advance. Don't waste mental energy on the day of the exam hunting for your bluebooks or car keys.

7. Sleep on it. Along with cramming, one of the big mistakes students make is loading up on caffeine or other stimulants to try to stay awake while studying. While these drugs may keep you up longer than usual, they often make you jittery or nervous as a side effect—not exactly the attitude you want heading into an exam. And eventually, you'll pay for the extra alertness with extra fatigue. The tale of the student who stayed up all night studying just to sleep through the exam is all too common. When you feel you have studied all you can, go to bed. The rest will help you to think better the next day.

8. Set two alarms. Be sure to get up early enough to take a shower, have a good breakfast, and look over your notes one last time before the test.

Works Cited

Robinson, Adam. *What Smart Students Know*. New York: Three Rivers Press, 1993.

Quick Tips for Taking Tests

If you haven't prepared well for a test or exam, no test-taking strategies will help you. However, even a well-prepared student can reduce nervousness and improve his or her performance by following these steps:

1. **Before going into an exam, review your notes one last time, if possible.** Remind yourself that you have prepared as well as you can and that you have every reason to feel confident taking this test.

2. **Review the entire test before beginning.** Note the kinds and numbers of questions and the weight given to each section. Read the instructions for each section and skim the questions to get an idea of difficulty—which ones will be easiest for you? Which ones will require the most effort? This is a good time to jot down on the back of a page any information you are worried about forgetting, such as dates or formulas.

3. **Answer the easiest questions first.** This will get you off to a quick start and will also help you build confidence for the more difficult questions.

4. **For multiple choice questions:**

   - See if you know the answer before looking at the choices.
   - Read all of your options before answering. Often there will be more than one answer that could fit—your task is to choose the best among them.
   - If you are unsure of the correct answer, try to eliminate the answers that you know to be incorrect. Then decide which of the remaining answers makes the most sense.

5. **For matching questions:**

   - Read both columns quickly.
   - Match the answers you are sure of first, and then use the process of elimination to determine the rest.

6. **For true-false questions:**

   - Read each statement carefully.
   - Make note of absolute terms such as "always" or "none." Often a statement that would otherwise be true is made false by one of these words.
   - Remember that if the statement is not completely true, it is false.

7. **For short-answer questions:**

   - Read the question carefully to be sure you understand what is required.
   - Answer the ones you know first.
   - Scan the rest of the test for clues if you get stuck. Although it is unlikely that the answer will appear somewhere else on the test, it's possible that another question may contain information that will jog your memory.

8. **For essay questions:**

   - Read the question carefully and be sure you understand it. A common mistake that students make when responding to essay questions is to simply begin writing everything they can think of on the topic. Look for key words such as "analyze," "compare," summarize," "describe" or "evaluate" that indicate what the professor wants you to do with the material.

- Answer the easy questions first.

- Plan your answer before you begin writing. If necessary, jot down a brief outline of the points you intend to make and the order in which you will present them.

- Keep an eye on the time. While it is important to write clearly and accurately, you do not have the luxury of editing and revising many times as you would on a take home essay. Try to write a clear and relatively thorough response to each question. If you finish before the end of the exam period, re-read and revise your answers for style.

- Make sure your answers are readable. Not only is printing easier to read, but it is quicker to write than cursive is. Bring an extra bluebook or paper so that you don't have to try to squeeze your answer into a cramped space. Use blue or black pen.

After the Exam

A good exam is more than just a test of what you know; it's also a learning experience in itself. Even before you get back your graded exam, you can assess your own performance. Did you study well? Were you informed about the kinds of questions that would be on the test and did you prepare accordingly? Did you organize your study materials effectively? Did your study group help prepare you for the exam or was it a distraction? What will you do differently next time?

When you receive your graded exam, don't just note the grade and put it away. Look it over to see how you can improve your studying and test-taking approach for the next test.

- Be sure the score is accurate. Even professors make mistakes. Always check the math and don't be afraid to politely point out an error. (Be sure to double-check your math before bringing the matter to your professor.)

- Read the professor's comments. If you are making the same type of error consistently, the professor may point this out to you. Jot down any questions you have about your professor's comments.

- Try to determine the cause of your mistakes. Was there a particular category of question that caused you trouble? Did you neglect to study a certain section of information? Did you misunderstand the question or fail to answer it completely?

- If you didn't do as well as you had hoped to, make an appointment to go over the test with your professor. Be sure to bring your test with you to the appointment and have two or three specific questions to ask. Your objective should not be to try to get the professor to change your grade, but rather to have him or her help you see what you need to do differently next time.

Test Anxiety

Have you ever experienced any of the following symptoms of test anxiety?

- Stomach ache or nausea prior to or during a test.

- Difficulty sleeping prior to a test.

- Sweaty palms, cold chills, or heart pounding during a test.

- Going blank on a test question, only to remember the answer once the test is over.

Being a little nervous prior to a big test can actually sharpen your senses and help you perform better. Some students, however, are prone to "test anxiety" an overwhelming sense of panic that overcomes them when they sit down to take a test. If you suffer from test anxiety, you may perform poorly no matter how carefully you have prepared.

Reducing Test Anxiety

Prior to the test:

- **Study smart.** Knowing that you have done all you can to prepare for the exam can give you confidence and reduce worry.

- **Exercise.** Regular exercise will help you feel better in general. A good aerobic workout the day before a test will also help you relax and sleep well that night.

- **Eat smart.** Don't skip meals or fill up on sugary snacks while studying and don't overdose on coffee. The same stimulants that helped you stay awake so you could study will leave you jittery and light-headed on exam day.

- **Get to class a few minutes early.** But avoid talking with other students; listening to their fears will only add to yours. Choose a good seat, arrange your materials, then walk down the hall, get a drink of water, and try to relax.

- **Try to sit toward the back of the room.** This way, you'll be able to see the whole class and won't be distracted, wondering what's going on behind you. It will also put you out of view of most of the class so that you won't feel self-conscious. This is especially important if you intend to use some kind of relaxation technique before or during the test.

During the Test

Before you begin the test, take a few moments to relax and rid yourself of negative thoughts and feelings. Try some of the following relaxation techniques:

- **Breathing.** Breathe in and out slowly nine times. Breathe deeply from your diaphragm and concentrate on breaths in and out. Visualize stress and anxiety flowing out each time you exhale.

- **Posture.** Don't slouch. Sit up straight in your chair with your shoulders back. Assume a position of confidence, even if you don't feel confident.

- **Positive thinking and affirmation.** Remind yourself of all you have done to prepare for this exam. Think about your past achievements and future goals. Tell yourself:

  I have studied hard, and I am prepared for this test.

  I am an intelligent person.

  I can achieve my goals.

  I can control my anxiety.

- **Take a break.** If you find yourself becoming anxious during the test, take a short break. Get a drink of water. Go to the bathroom. Use the time away from the test to relax and refocus.

- **Don't rush.** Work at a steady pace and don't worry about what other students are doing.

- **Accept the worst case.** If all else fails and you just don't see anyway that you can pass this test, accept that fact! Adam Robinson suggests the following strategy:

  Now look for the easiest question on the test, a question you know you can do. Say to yourself, 'Well, I know I'm going to fail, but at least I can do this question.' Once you've answered that question, look for another easy one you can do. Focusing on answering the questions takes your mind off failure, and answer by answer you will gradually get your confidence back (186).

Most students experience test anxiety at one time or another in their academic careers. If you have trouble getting your test anxiety under control, make an appointment to talk to a counselor in the counseling center.

Works Cited

Robinson, Adam. *What Smart Students Know.* New York: Three Rivers Press, 1993.

My College Journey

George Gallagher, Professor of Animal Science

As with many students, I was struggling with college trying to attend classes, read, study and work two jobs. I spent many hours and all-nighters working hard to maintain C's. Early in my sophomore year the light bulbs went off. I was training horses at the time and after a particularly good session with a mare, I got off and went through my mental checklist of techniques utilized, categorizing why some did or did not work with this particular animal. It suddenly dawned on me that I needed to study the same way I trained horses. The concept is simple. To learn a new task effectively requires short-term highly intensive time periods with sufficient repetition and frequency as reinforcement. In other words it takes practice and repetition. Second, some techniques work better for some individuals and are less effective for others.

I developed a set of study notes for each class. Outlining book chapters and updating my study notes was accomplished between classes. My study sessions occurred every evening and consisted of two or three intense 30-minute periods, each followed by a short break. I also learned the importance of eating and sleeping habits. I learned never to study past 10:00 pm and never look at material the day of the test. What was the outcome? My hours spent studying actually decreased while my understanding and appreciation of the material, not to mention grades, skyrocketed. Sometimes it pays to listen to animals or at least not ignore the obvious. Think about it, can a puppy learn to sit in five hours? The answer is yes, but not in one afternoon. Are we really that much different?

GETTING ALONG WITH PROFESSORS

Professors: Who Are They and What Do They Do?

Dale McConkey

Chaplain and Associate Professor of Sociology

There's something about the term "college professor" that often evokes a sense of respect, even awe. In survey after survey, the American public ranks college professors as the third most prestigious occupation, just behind doctors and lawyers. At the same time, however, college professors (like doctors and lawyers) are often the focus of playful ridicule and the butt of many jokes. Our society sympathetically laughs at the "absent-minded professor" and disapprovingly scoffs at the "ivory-tower professor" who blindly lives in the world of abstract ideas and fails to demonstrate any "street smarts."

Exactly who are professors? This is an important question, for you will have about five of them as your "boss" each semester. It is always useful to know the personality and characteristics of the people who have some level of authority over you. Certainly, it is not possible to pigeon-hole all professors into a single description, but professors have gone through a similar set of experiences that might help you understand whom you will be dealing with for the next four years or so. Perhaps the best way to describe college professors is to compare them to your high-school teachers.

College professors are extensively trained in a particular topic, not the profession of teaching. Another way of saying this is that college professors are trained in a topic to teach, rather than a process of teaching. Almost all high-school teachers, even those with master's or doctoral degrees, have been taught how to teach. They learn the process of teaching: how to communicate information, maintain students' attention, and create lesson plans. College professors, in contrast, often have no formal training in teaching methods. Instead, they are thoroughly trained in particular subject matter. Their degrees are each in a specific field (sociology, for example), but they almost always specialize in an even more narrow subfield (like criminology). Even within the subfield, your professors have carved out a little niche of their own (like the murder patterns of one-eyed Norwegian walrus salesmen—not quite that esoteric and obscure, but close). Thus, professors are specialists in specific subject matter; the amount of training they have received in teaching methods will vary greatly.

What Do College Professors Actually Do?

You know what college students do: take about five courses, study for each one, work at a side job, and try to maintain some type of social life. But what about college professors? How do they fill up their work week? Unlike your high-school instructors, your college professors spend only about twelve hours per week inside the classroom. Does this mean that they have a cushy job? Not at all. Like any profession, you will find the occasional professor who is just "getting by" on minimal work. Most professors, however, work very hard for their money. Here are some tasks professors perform in addition to teaching in the classroom:

- **Prepare classes.** Just as students are expected to spend two hours studying for every one hour of class time, so, too, are professors expected to spend considerable time preparing high-quality lectures and guided discussions. Experienced professors may be seasoned enough to spend less time (then they are expected to contribute to more of the tasks below), but newly-hired professors might spend three or four hours preparing a single lecture.

- **Serve the college.** Professors are expected to contribute not only to the smooth running of their classes, but also to the smooth operation of the college as a whole. This expectation includes tasks such as sponsoring student clubs, organizations, and events; serving on college committees (and there are lots of them); and developing innovative ideas for the institutional development of the college. In any case, professors must serve the college beyond the confines of their classes.

- **Continue scholarly research.** Not only are professors expected to contribute to students (through teaching) and to the college (through committees), but they are also required to serve their specific academic discipline (e.g., history, biology, economics, etc.). Professors do this by writing scholarly books and articles. It requires a significant amount of time and energy to read and keep current on the significant developments in one's chosen field, and even more effort to produce new contributions to the discipline.

These three categories—*teaching, service, and scholarship*—comprise the major components of your professors' job responsibilities. Performing these tasks well is essential if the professor is to receive tenure (see the section below, "What do all the titles mean?").

What Do All the Titles Mean?

Teachers are teachers, right? Well, sort of. Just like any profession, the academic world has a "ladder" of status, with your teachers standing on various rungs. In practice, you will probably not notice this status hierarchy (After all, you need to respect all of the teachers.), but it still might be helpful to understand the differences.

A key distinction is whether a teacher has a terminal degree, the highest possible academic degree that can be held for his or her chosen area of study. The most frequent terminal degree is a Ph.D. (doctor of philosophy); also included are the Ed.D. (doctor of education), the D.B.A. (doctor of business administration), the D.M.A. (doctor of musical arts), and others.

If the teacher does not have a terminal degree, she or he is usually either a lecturer, someone who has no immediate intentions of earning a terminal degree, or an instructor, someone who may soon earn a Ph.D. or equivalent. After the teacher receives a terminal degree, he or she usually earns the rank of assistant professor, described below.

Most of your teachers at Berry (around 90 percent) have earned a terminal degree. These people are usually referred to as professors (not teachers), and they go by "Dr." (not "Ms." or "Mr."). There are three levels of professors: assistant professors, associate professors, and full professors. Assistant professors have the lowest rank and are usually the newest professors. Full professors have the highest rank and experience, with associate professors between these two.

Another key distinction among your professors is whether they have received tenure. Tenure is a grueling process that professors (not instructors or lecturers) encounter during the sixth year of service to a college or university. At that time, the professor provides a lengthy report on her or his teaching in the classroom, service to the college, and scholarship in the relevant discipline. If the college awards tenure to a professor, he or she is given an enhanced level of job security. If the person does not receive tenure, she or he may apply again the following year. After twice failing to receive tenure in a row, a professor must seek employment elsewhere.

With a minimum of ten years of service at Berry, a professor who retires is usually awarded the title "Professor Emeritus."

Courses: What Are Professors Trying to Accomplish?

You are spending about fifteen hours every week sitting in a desk, listening to professors wax eloquent (i.e., speak articulately) about a variety of topics. You are taking notes on hundreds—perhaps thousands—of details. What's the point? How do all these details fit together? Why are we studying this stuff, anyway? Good questions. It is always helpful to take a moment, step back, and look at the "big picture." What are professors trying to do when they are professing?

Here are four goals professors often cite:

1. **Provide the "nuts and bolts" of the subject matter.** College is the place where great thoughts are born, where new ideas blossom, and where great intellectual debates rage. Before all these lofty endeavors can be reasonably pursued, it is first essential to acquire a basic foundation of knowledge. This foundation comprises most of your general-education (gen-ed) courses, which normally consumes most of your first two years. Your gen-ed professors will spend a considerable amount of time feeding you facts for your memorization pleasure. Some of you will gripe and complain about the uselessness of knowing the color of George Washington's white horse, but seemingly insignificant facts such as these can eventually add up to a coherent body of knowledge. Just as beautiful mosaics are created out of thousands and thousands of apparently insignificant and unrelated tile, so, too, is your complete college education based upon an understanding of many detailed facts. In other words, facts are the building blocks that allow one to develop critical, theoretical, and philosophical arguments. Without first

having a substantial foundation of facts, your theories and philosophies are not much more sophisticated than talk-show rhetoric.

2. **See the "big picture" of a discipline.** Just as theories without facts are useless and uninformed, facts without theories are boring bundles of balderdash. Once you learn the essential content of an academic discipline, most of your professors will be eager to take you to the "next step" and encourage you to answer the ultimate academic question: So what? So what if the income gap is higher in industrial countries than in preindustrial ones? So what if female rats get aggressive when they are injected with male testosterone? So what if you have a photo of Elvis swimming in Loch Ness with Big Foot? Your professors will eventually encourage you to make sense of the myriad of facts and data that are now hopefully embedded in your brain. Certainly you will be challenged in this way in your upper-level courses, but you will also experience a substantial amount of critical, "big picture" thinking in your gen-ed courses.

3. **Develop a love of topic and a zest for independent thinking and research.** Another academic irony: professors are perhaps most excited about their teaching when they teach a student who no longer needs them. As previously stated, professors are in love with their subject matter. You can only imagine how it feels when they find a student (an apprentice, really) who shares that passion for the topic. It is this type of student who begins to ask her or his own questions—and seek her or his own answers. When students develop the ability to ask the right questions and then demonstrate the competence to seek out the possible answers without the aid of the professor, that professor has done her or his job. Just as parents feel a sense of accomplishment when their child leaves the nest and thrives without their help, so, too, do professors cherish students who share a yearning for knowledge.

4. **Link the knowledge gained from class to the reality of life.** Knowledge and learning are wonderful pursuits, but there is something slightly short-sighted and self-indulgent about the person who learns only for the sake of learning. Even the most utopian idealist will tell you that knowledge is a tool to be used; in our postindustrial, information-oriented society, this need to put knowledge into practice is more important today than at any time in history. The knowledge you possess (and the problem-solving, critical-thinking skills that develop along with it) will certainly be useful in the professions you pursue. Most professors, however, will go one step further and declare that there is something even more fundamentally useful about knowledge than simple career advancement. Simply put, knowledge should promote personal growth and maturity.

It is nice to know things to know them; but the ability to utilize them, to recognize them, to apply them, is even greater than wonderful.
—Dan McBrayer, Dana Professor of Education and Psychology

Perhaps more than at any other time in your life, college affords you the opportunity to examine yourself—your beliefs, your values, your core identity. If you are not allowing the information you are acquiring in college to challenge you at the essence of your being, you are missing an opportunity that rarely surfaces later in life. This does not mean that professors expect you to abandon your previous worldview in favor of another. It does, however, mean that if you do maintain your original beliefs, you will have challenged and explored them until you have a deeper, richer understanding of them. As Socrates said, "The unexamined life is not worth living."

What Should You Expect From Professors?

Respect

Your professor-student relationship is a relationship between two adults. Your professor should treat you accordingly. That does not mean you will have equal footing with your professors. They have a level of authority that you don't, and this requires them to (1) demand a certain level of work out of you and (2) to evaluate this work. Nevertheless, your professor should always treat you respectfully as an active participant in your own education.

Accessibility

Professors normally are required to be in their offices available to students for ten hours or more per week. This is substantially more required office time than professors at large universities typically hold, where they may be in their office only two hours per week or less. If you are having trouble making it to your professors' posted office hours, tell them, and they will, in all likelihood, be more than willing to schedule an appointment for another time.

Intellectual Sharpness

You should always expect that professors will come to class well prepared and ready to teach. Furthermore, you should expect that they be well informed on the most recent trends in their respective discipline, which requires ongoing scholarly activity.

Commitment to Learning

Regardless of the course or topic, your professors should be willing to do whatever it takes to assist the consistently motivated student to learn and understand the material at hand.

Challenging But Fair Standards

One of your favorite pastimes at college will be griping about the amount of work you have to do and the dastardly professors who assigned such a ridiculous amount of work. "Don't they realize we have four other classes and a job?" "Don't they want us to have a life?" We professors have heard it all. At the same time, we have heard students gripe at length about the professors who were lax and unchallenging to such an extent that the students didn't learn anything. Deep down, we all know that college should challenge us; it should make us push our limits and stimulate personal growth. Professors strive for this to happen. At the same time, if the requirements are too stringent, panic and paralysis will supplant personal growth. Professors normally find a proper balance somewhere in between having unrealistic expectations and having unchallenging ones.

What Professors Expect of You

Engagement

Woody Allen's famous observation that "80% of success is just showing up" does not apply in college. Certainly, your professors expect you to be in class, and to arrive promptly, but they expect a great deal more than your mere presence. Professors expect you to come prepared for class. They assume that you have done any assigned reading and are prepared to participate in a discussion or to follow a lecture that builds on ideas or information in the text. Professors don't mind answering questions or clarifying passages that may have confused you, but will resent your taking up class time to ask for basic information that you should have gained from your reading or from previous classes. It should go without saying that professors also expect you to be attentive in class. Whispering to other students or working on an assignment for another class is not just distracting, it's disrespectful to both the professor and your classmates.

Responsibility

Professors expect you to be active participants in your own learning. In addition to coming prepared to and engaging in every class, they also expect you to pursue help if you run into difficulty. At Berry, every professor keeps regular office hours; they expect you to take advantage of these office hours to seek help understanding difficult concepts or to get feedback on papers and other assignments. They will probably not, however, seek you out. As an adult, you are expected to take the initiative.

A Serious Approach to Work

Take care in preparing the work that you submit. Dog-eared pages and numerous mechanical errors suggest a sloppy attitude toward the work itself. Likewise, comments in class that don't reflect serious thought or engagement will not be appreciated.

Honesty

Professors know that students have lives outside the classroom and that circumstances will occasionally occur that warrant a student's missing class or turning in an assignment late, and most are willing to extend deadlines or arrange make-up tests to accommodate legitimate requests. Professors will not respect excessive excuses for chronic absences or tardy work, however, and they will not tolerate lying or cheating. If you need help, ask for it. If you've failed to do the work you should have, accept the consequences of your choices.

Assertiveness

Assertiveness is a valued trait in college. So long as it is done respectfully, professors welcome you to challenge material they or your textbooks present as it shows that you are thinking critically about your studies. Professors also welcome your questions and concerns about your grades. Professors are only human and occasionally make errors; if you can demonstrate that a mistake has been made, they will be glad to correct it. More frequently, however, they will help you understand why they graded your work as they did. Asking a professor to go over your test or paper with you and explain his or her grading is a good learning opportunity.

As you look back over this list, you'll notice that at the heart of each of these expectations is a presumption of mutual respect. Professors will treat you as mature individuals and will expect you to act as such.

Those Winter Sundays

Robert Hayden

Poet

When Robert Hayden (1913–1980) was three years old, his mother, wanting more inde-
pendence, gave him to another couple to raise. Hayden grew up in poverty in Detroit, joined
the WPA Federal Writer's Project in the 1930s, and eventually studied English at the Uni-
versity of Michigan under the poet W. H. Auden. A widely published poet, Hayden also
taught at Fisk University in Nashville and at the University of Michigan. In this poem,
Hayden seems to be reflecting on his relationship with his adoptive father. As you read it,
think about your own past relationships with parents, teachers, or other mentors.

Sundays, too, my father got up early and
put his clothes on in the blueblack cold,
then with cracked hands that ached
from labor in the weekday weather made
banked fires blaze. No one ever thanked him.

I'd wake and hear the cold splintering, breaking.
When the rooms were warm, he'd call,
and slowly I would rise and dress,
fearing the chronic angers of that house.

Speaking indifferently to him,
who had driven out the cold
and polished my good shoes as well.
What did I know,
what did I know
of love's austere and lonely offices?

The 'Banked Fires' of Robert Hayden's "Those Winter Sundays"

David Huddle

Poet and Fiction Writer

David Huddle is a poet and fiction writer who teaches at the University of Vermont and the Bread Loaf School of English. In this essay, Huddle describes his approach to teaching one of his favorite poems, "Those Winter Sundays" by Robert Hayden. As you read this piece, pay attention to the various considerations that inform Huddle's classroom presentation. Think about the advance preparation that both you and your professors do for the classes you're currently taking.

For twenty years I've been teaching Robert Hayden's most frequently anthologized poem to undergraduate poetry-writing students. By "teach," I mean that from our textbook I read the poem aloud in the classroom, I ask one of the students to read it aloud, I make some observations about it, I invite the students to make some observations about it, then we talk about it a while longer. Usually to wrap up the discussion, I'll read the poem through once more. Occasions for such teaching come up about half a dozen times a year, and so let's say that during my life I've been privileged to read this poem aloud approximately 240 times. "Those Winter Sundays" has withstood my assault upon it. It remains a poem I look forward to reading and discussing in my classroom. The poem remains alive to me, so that for hours and sometimes days after it visits my classroom, I'm hearing its lines in my mind's ear.

Though a fourteen-liner, "Those Winter Sundays" is only loosely a sonnet. Its stanzas are five, four, and five lines long. There are rhymes and near-rhymes, but no rhyme scheme. The poem's lines probably average about eight syllables. There are only three strictly iambic lines: the fourth, the eighth, and (significantly) the fourteenth. It's a poem that's powerfully informed by the sonnet form; it's a poem that "feels like" a sonnet—it has the density and gravity of a sonnet—which is to say that in its appearance on the page, in its diction and syntax, in its tone, cadence, and argumentative strategy, "Those Winter Sundays" presents the credentials of a work of literary art in the tradition of English letters. But it's also a poem that has gone its own way, a definite departure from that most conventional of all the poetic forms of English and American verse.

The abstract issue of this poem's sonnethood is of less value to my beginning poets than the tangible matter of the sounds the poem makes, especially those k-sounding words of the first eleven lines that one comes to associate with discomfort: "clothes. . . blueblack cold. . . cracked. . . ached. . . weekday. . . banked. . . thanked. . . wake. . .

cold. . . breaking. . . call. . . chronic. . . cold." What's missing from the final three lines? The *k* sounds have been driven from the poem, as the father has "driven out the cold" from the house. The sounds that have replaced those *k* sounds are the *o* sounds of "good. . . shoes. . . know. . . know. . . love. . . lonely offices." The poem lets us associate the *o* sounds with love and loneliness. Sonically the poem tells the same story the poem narrates for us. The noise of this poem moves us through its emotional journey from discomfort to lonely love. If ever there was a poem that could teach a beginning poet the viability of the element of sound-crafting, it is "Those Winter Sundays."

Quote its first two words, and a great many poets and English teachers will be able to finish the first line (if not the whole poem) from memory. Somewhat remarkably, the poem's thesis—that the office of love can be relentless, thankless, and more than a little mysterious—resides in that initially odd-sounding two-word beginning, "Sundays too." The rest of the line—the rest of the independent clause—is ordinary. Nowhere else in Anglo-American literature does the word *too* carry the weight it carries in "Those Winter Sundays."

Not as immediately apparent as its opening words but very nearly as important to the poem's overall strategy is the two-sentence engineering of the first stanza. Because they will appreciate it more if they discover it for themselves, I often maneuver Socratically to have my students describe the poem's first two sentences: long and complex, followed by short and simple. It almost always seems to me worthwhile to ask, "Why didn't Hayden begin his poem this way: 'No one ever thanked my father for getting up early on Sundays, too'? Wouldn't that be a more direct and hospitable way to bring the reader into the poem?" After I've taken my students that far, they are quick to see how that ordinary five-word unit, "No one ever thanked him," gains meaning and emotion, weight, and force, from the elaborate preparation given it by the thirty-two word "Sundays too" first sentence.

So much depends on "No one ever thanked him" that it requires the narrative enhancement of the first four and a half lines. It is the crux of the poem. What is this poem about? It is about a son's remorse over never thanking his father not only for what he did for him but also for how (he now realizes) he felt about him. And what is the poem if not an elegantly fashioned, permanent expression of gratitude?

"Those Winter Sundays" tells a story, or it describes a circumstance, of father-son conflict, and it even makes some excuses for the son's "Speaking indifferently" to the father: there was a good deal of anger between them; "chronic angers of that house" suggests that the circumstances were complicated somewhat beyond the usual and ordinary conflict between fathers and sons. Of the father, we know that he labored outdoors with his hands. Of the son, we know that he was, in the classic manner of youth, heedless of the ways in which his father served him.

Though the evidence of his "labor" is visible in every stanza of this poem, the father himself is somewhere else. We don't see him. He is in some other room of the house than the one where our speaker is. That absence suggests the emotional distance between the father and the son as well as the current absence, through death, of the father on the occasion of this utterance. It's easy enough to imagine this poem as a graveside meditation, an elegy, and a rather impassioned one at that, "What did I know, what did I know?"

The grinding of past against present gives the poem its urgency. The story is being told with such clarity, thoughtfulness, and apparent calm that we are surprised by the outburst of the repeated question of the thirteenth line. The fourteenth line returns to a tone of tranquillity. Its diction is formal, even arch, and its phrasing suggests an extremely considered conclusion; the fourteenth line is the answer to a drastic rephrasing of the original question: What is the precise name of what as a youth I was incapable of perceiving but that as a life-examining adult, I now suddenly understand?

I tell my students that they may someday need this poem, they may someday be walking along downtown and find themselves asking aloud, "What did I know, what did I know?" But what I mean to suggest to them is that Hayden has made them the gift of this final phrase like a package that in ten years' time they may open and find immensely valuable: "love's austere and lonely offices." Like "the banked fires" his father made, Hayden has made a poem that will be of value to readers often years after they've first read it.

"Those Winter Sundays" has articulated a treasure of an insight and preserved it for me until I was old enough to appreciate it. The poem always has the power to move me, to make me understand something so subtle that apparently I need to be reminded of it again and again. Hayden's poem is a "banked fire" that holds its warmth and allows me to rekindle my spirits whenever I come back to read it.

"Those Winter Sundays" honors a much-criticized figure in American culture of the 1990s—the withdrawn, emotionally inexpressive, and distant (and probably unhappy and angry) father. The poem makes its way toward perceiving the emotional life of such a man. The poem realizes love as it lived in such a man. That my own father was somewhat similar is perhaps why the poem particularly affects me, but I have witnessed its affecting so many others that I must assume either that such fathers exist in multitudes or that the poem cuts across vast differences of background in its instruction to the reader to reconsider the lives of those who helped us make our way into adulthood.

Whenever I teach "Those Winter Sundays," I face a dilemma of personal, political, and pedagogical consequence. Do I tell my students that Hayden is an African-American poet? That fact does make a difference in how we read the poem: the "cracked hands that ached / from labor in the weekday weather" may be seen in a context of a racial-economic circumstance, and thus "the chronic angers of that house" may also be seen as a result of racially enforced poverty. There are, however, laborers and poor families of all ethnic backgrounds, and so one need not necessarily read "Those Winter Sundays" as a poem that has anything to do with racial issues. It might even be argued that to read the poem as being about race is to give the poem a racist reading.

My students are almost always white, they are only beginning to learn about modern poetry, and they aren't likely to be acquainted with any African-American poets. If I tell them that Hayden was an African American, am I practicing a subtly racist bit of pedagogy? On the other hand, if I don't tell them that the man who wrote this poem is African-American, aren't I denying them a piece of knowledge that is essential not only for the understanding of this poem but for their general poetic education? (One wonders what the equivalent might be for another poet—to omit telling students of a Robert Frost poem that he lived most of his life in New England? To say nothing about Walt Whitman's homosexuality? To leave unmentioned Emily Dickinson's reclusiveness? Is there really any equivalent?)

I'm a teacher; I almost always look for a positive approach to such dilemmas. I see an admirable ambiguity and psychological complexity in the fact that the poem can be read in both ways, as a poem that is somewhat informed by the circumstance of racial injustice. I do tell my students that the author was an African-American, but I tell them only after we've read it a couple of times and talked about it. That piece of information is very nearly the last thing that I tell them before I read it to them the last time, the reading in which once more I journey in my own voice through the words, the lines, the stanzas, down through the cold house into the waiting warmth it always offers me, that necessary, inspiring insight it delivers to me again and again, that the duties of love (like the duties of poetry) are often scrupulously carried out in invisible and thankless ways.

Re-reading Questions

1. Find the specific passages in this essay in which Huddle talks about the choices he makes as a teacher. How does Huddle define "teaching" in the first paragraph and elsewhere? How does his definition of teaching confirm or differ with your understanding of that task?

2. What is the thesis of Hayden's poem, according to Huddle? Do you agree?

3. What does Huddle mean when he says he faces a "dilemma of personal, political, and psychological consequence" when deciding whether or not to tell his students that Hayden is African-American? Do you agree that this information is as significant as he seems to think it is? What do you think of his solution to the dilemma?

Discussion Questions

1. In paragraph 5, Huddle says he "maneuver[s] Socratically" to lead his students to discover the structure of Hayden's opening stanza for themselves. Why is it important that they discover that structure themselves? Thinking about your own learning experiences, do you have a preference for classes that are discussion-based or lecture-based? Do you find that some subjects lend themselves to one or another approach? Thinking about the courses you are taking this semester, in which of them would you say the instructor is trying to lead you to discover ideas for yourself? In which do you think the instructor is presenting ideas directly to you?

2. Discuss the significance of Huddle's final sentence as it applies to both Hayden's poem and Huddle's essay.

Discovery Questions

1. Huddle's essay offers insight into the mind and work of one college professor, and suggests that much of what teachers do is unnoticed by their students. Choose one of your professors and schedule a few minutes to talk to him or her about teaching. Use these questions to guide your interview: Ask him or her to think of a topic, lesson, piece, or skill he or she particularly enjoys teaching. Ask what preparations he or she makes to teach that particular lesson. What problems (pedagogical, psychological, political, personal, or other) does he or she face in trying to teach? How does he or she attempt to address those problems? What does he or she find most rewarding about teaching that lesson or about teaching in general? Be prepared to discuss your findings at your next seminar meeting.

2. Write an essay similar to Huddle's from a student's perspective. What are the "austere and lonely offices" of a student? Think of a course or another learning experience that was or is important to you. Write about the unseen preparation and work that you put into that experience. What problems or difficulties does/did the experience present? How do you or did you handle those problems?

MAKING THE GRADE

Academic Goals for First Semester

As you approach mid-term of your first semester, take a minute to refer back to the academic goals you set at the beginning of the year.

Target cumulative GPA at the end of this semester _____.

Course	Mid-term grade	Credits	Grade points (credits × grade value*)
TOTALS			
Midterm GPA (Total grade points /total credits)			

*Grade Value: **A** 4.0, **A−** 3.7, **B+** 3.3, **B** 3, **B−** 2.7, **C+** 2.3, **C** 5, **C−** 1.7, **D+** 1.3, **D** 1, **F** 0

Which course are you finding to be the easiest for you? Why? Is it the course that you predicted would be easiest?

Which course do you find to be the most difficult? Why? Is it the course that you predicted would be the most difficult?

Consider the list of three things you planned to do in your most difficult course at the beginning of the semester. How successful have you been actually doing those three things?

Consider the list you made at the beginning of the semester of three behaviors to bring you closer to your desired GPA. How successful have you been at actually carrying out those behaviors?

Do the goals you set for yourself at the beginning of the semester seem realistic and attainable at this point? If not, how would you modify them?

Academic Integrity

From the Berry College Catalog

The Berry College community affirms its support of academic integrity as reflecting founder Martha Berry's commitment to educating the head, heart, and hands, and as the foundation of college life and experience. We believe that mutual trust among Berry's students, faculty, and staff is essential to the operation of the college and that all members of the Berry College community are responsible for working together to establish and uphold an environment conducive to honorable academic endeavor.

Academic dishonesty includes, *but is not limited to*, the following: cheating, unauthorized collaboration, plagiarism, fabrication, multiple submissions, and aiding and abetting;

Cheating: using or providing unauthorized information or aids on any examination or other graded assignment; altering a graded work prior to its return to a faculty member; doing another's work or allowing another person to do one's work, and submitting it for grading;

Unauthorized Collaboration: working with another person on a project, assignment, examination, test, or quiz, unless collaborative work has been stipulated by the instructor;

Plagiarism: submitting material that in part or whole is not one's own work without properly attributing the source(s) of its content;

Fabrication: inventing or falsifying information, data, or citations; altering or creating any document or record affecting the grade or academic standing of oneself or others;

Multiple Submissions: submitting identical or substantially similar papers or course work for credit in more than one course without prior permission of the instructor(s);

Aiding and Abetting: providing material, information, or other assistance which violates any of the above standards for academic integrity; providing false information in connection with any inquiry regarding academic integrity.

Where there is a suspected violation of academic integrity policy, the concerned faculty member should:

(a) discuss the suspected infraction directly with the student(s) involved. At the faculty member's or student's discretion, the school dean, department chair, or faculty colleague may be present during this discussion as a witness;

(b) make copies of relevant materials before returning them to the student(s) for any approved amendment or revision;

(c) discuss the suspected infraction and the documented evidence with the department chair, dean, or a colleague if collegial advice is desired. In all such cases, the privacy of the student(s) involved must be protected;

(d) make a decision based on the evidence and determine appropriate sanctions; sanctions may include warning the student, or reducing an assignment, exam, or course grade; if sanctions are imposed, discuss these and the appeals process with the student;

(e) if a student is found to have violated academic integrity policy, notify the provost (or associate provost) in writing. This document should include:

1. information about the course, the faculty involved, and the student(s) involved;

2. the time and date of the incident, and a description of the incident and any evidence that indicates an infraction of academic integrity;

3. any sanctions imposed by the faculty member in response to this incident; and

4. a confirmation that the faculty member has discussed with the student the incident, any sanctions imposed, and the student's right to appeal the faculty member's decision.

Students seeking to appeal the sanction concerning academic integrity may appeal to a subcommittee consisting of equal numbers of faculty and students of the Graduate Council, which will be convened by the provost or associate provost.

Students who are sanctioned for violating academic integrity policy forfeit the right to withdraw from the class with a grade of "W."

Integrity

Stephen L. Carter

William Nelson Cromwell Professor of Law at Yale University

Stephen L. Carter is the William Nelson Cromwell Professor of Law at Yale University. In this excerpt from his book Integrity *Carter expresses dismay over our culture's indifference toward—and lack of understanding of—personal integrity. As you read, consider ways in which integrity will be crucial during your college career.*

My first lesson in integrity came the hard way. It was 1960 or thereabouts and I was a first-grader at P.S. 129 in Harlem. The teacher had us all sitting in a circle, playing a game in which each child would take a turn donning a blindfold and then trying to identify objects by touch alone as she handed them to us. If you guessed right, you stayed in until the next round. If you guessed wrong, you were out. I survived almost to the end, amazing the entire class with my abilities. Then, to my dismay, the teacher realized what I had known, and relied upon, from the start: my blindfold was tied imperfectly and a sliver of bright reality leaked in from outside. By holding the unknown object in my lap instead of out in front of me, as most of the other children did, I could see at least a corner or a side and sometimes more—but always enough to figure out what it was. So my remarkable success was due only to my ability to break the rules.

Fortunately for my own moral development, I was caught. And as a result of being caught, I suffered, in front of my classmates, a humiliating reminder of right and wrong: I had cheated at the game. Cheating was wrong. It was that simple.

I do not remember many of the details of the "public" lecture that I received from my teacher. I do remember that I was made to feel terribly ashamed; and it is good that I was made to feel that way, for I had something to be ashamed of. The moral opprobrium that accompanied that shame was sufficiently intense that it has stayed with me ever since, which is exactly how shame is supposed to work. And as I grew older, whenever I was even tempted to cheat—at a game, on homework—I would remember my teacher's stern face and the humiliation of sitting before my classmates, revealed to the world as a cheater.

That was then, this is now. Browsing recently in my local bookstore, I came across a book that boldly proclaimed, on its cover, that it contained instructions on how to cheat—the very word occurred in the title—at a variety of video games. My instincts tell me that this cleverly chosen title is helping the book to sell very well, for it captures precisely what is wrong with America today: we care far more about winning than about playing by the rules.

Consider just a handful of examples, drawn from headlines of the mid-1990s: the winner of the Miss Virginia pageant is stripped of her title after officials determine that her educational credentials are false; a television network is forced to apologize for using explosives to add a bit of verisimilitude to a tape purporting to show that a particular truck is unsafe; and the authors of a popular book on management are accused of using bulk purchases at key stores to manipulate the *New York Times* best-seller list. Go back a few more years and we can add everything from a slew of Wall Street titans imprisoned for violating a bewildering variety of laws in their frantic effort to get ahead, to the women's Boston Marathon winner branded a cheater for spending part of the race on the subway. But cheating is evidently no big deal: some 70 percent of college students admit to having done it at least once.

That, in a nutshell, is America's integrity dilemma: we are full of fine talk about how desperately our society needs it, but, when push comes to shove, we would just as soon be on the winning side. A couple of years ago I sat watching a televised football game with my children, trying to explain to them what was going on. I was struck by an event I had often noticed but on which I had never reflected. A player who failed to catch a ball thrown his way hit the ground, rolled over, and then jumped up, celebrating as though he had caught the pass after all. The referee was standing in a position that did not give him a good view of what had happened, was fooled by the player's pretense, and so moved the ball down the field. The player rushed back to the huddle so that his team could run another play before the officials had time to review the tape. (Until 1992, National Football League officials could watch a television replay and change their call as long as the next play had not been run.) But viewers at home did have the benefit of the replay, and we saw what the referee missed: the ball lying on the ground instead of snug in the receiver's hands. The only comment from the broadcasters: "What a heads-up play!" Meaning: "Wow, what a great liar this kid is! Well done!

Let's be very clear: that is exactly what they meant. The player set out to mislead the referee and succeeded; he helped his team to obtain an advantage in the game that it had not earned. It could not have been accidental. He knew he did not catch the ball. By jumping up and celebrating, he was trying to convey a false impression. He was trying to convince the officials that he had caught the ball. And the officials believed him. So, in any ordinary understanding of the word, he lied. And that, too, is what happens to integrity in American life: if we happen to do something wrong, we would just as soon have nobody point it out.

Now, suppose that the player had instead gone to the referee and said, "I'm sorry, sir, but I did not make the catch. Your call is wrong." Probably his coach and teammates and most of his team's fans would have been furious; he would not have been a good team player. The good team player lies to the referee and does so in a manner that is at once blatant (because millions of viewers see it) and virtually impossible for the referee to detect. Having pulled off this trickery, the player is congratulated. He is told that he has made a heads-up play. Thus, the ethic of the game turns out to be an ethic that rewards cheating. (But I still love football.) Perhaps I should have been shocked. Yet, thinking through the implications of our celebration of a national sport that rewards cheating, I could not help but recognize that we as a nation too often lack integrity, which might be described in a loose and colloquial way, as the courage of one's convictions. And although I do not want to claim any great burst of inspiration, it was at about that time that I decided to write this book.

Toward a Definition

We, the People of the United States, who a little over two hundred years ago ordained and established the Constitution, have a serious problem: too many of us nowadays neither mean what we say nor say what we mean. Moreover, we hardly expect anybody else to mean what they say either.

A couple of years ago I began a university commencement address by telling the audience that I was going to talk about integrity. The crowd broke into applause. Applause! Just because they had heard the word integrity—that's how starved for it they were. They had no idea how I was using the word, or what I was going to say about it, or, indeed, whether I was for it or against it. But they knew they liked the idea of simply talking about it. This celebration of integrity is intriguing. We seem to carry on a passionate love affair with a word that we scarcely pause to define.

The Supreme Court likes to use such phrases as the "Constitution's structural integrity" when it strikes down actions that violate the separation of powers in the federal government. Critics demand a similar form of integrity when they argue that our age has seen the corruption of language or of particular religious traditions or of the moral sense generally. Indeed, when parents demand a form of education that will help their children grow into people of integrity, the cry carries a neo-romantic image of their children becoming adults who will remain uncorrupted by the forces (whatever they are) that seem to rob so many grown-ups of. . . well, of integrity.

Very well, let us consider this word integrity. Integrity is like the weather— everybody talks about it but nobody knows what to do about it. Integrity is that stuff we always say we want more of. Such leadership gurus as Warren Bennis insist that it is of first importance. We want our elected representatives to have it, and political challengers always insist that their opponents lack it. We want it in our spouses, our children, our friends. We want it in our schools and our houses of worship. And in our corporations and the products they manufacture: early in 1995, one automobile company widely advertised a new car as "the first concept car with integrity." And we want it in the federal government, too, where officials all too frequently find themselves under investigation by special prosecutors. So perhaps we should say that integrity is like good weather because everybody is in favor of it.

Scarcely a politician kicks off a campaign without promising to bring it to government; a few years later, more often than is healthy for our democracy, the politician slinks cravenly from office, having been lambasted by the press for lacking that self-same integrity; and then the press, in turn, is skewered for holding public figures to a measure of integrity that its own reporters, editors, producers, and, most particularly, owners could not possibly meet. And for refusing to turn that critical eye inward, the press is mocked for—what else? A lack of integrity.

Everybody agrees that the nation needs more of it. Some say we need to return to the good old days when we had a lot more of it. Others say we as a nation have never really had enough of it. And hardly any of us stop to explain exactly what we mean by it, or how we know it is even a good thing, or why everybody needs to have the same amount of it. Indeed, the only trouble with integrity is that everybody who uses the word seems to mean something slightly different. So in a book about integrity, the place to start is surely with a definition.

When I refer to integrity, I have something very simple and very specific in mind. Integrity, as I will use the term, requires three steps:

1. discerning what is right and what is wrong;

2. acting on what you have discerned, even at personal cost; and

3. saying openly that you are acting on your understanding of right from wrong

The first criterion captures the idea of integrity as requiring a degree of moral reflectiveness. The second brings in the ideal of an integral person as steadfast, which includes the sense of keeping commitments. The third reminds us that a person of integrity is unashamed of doing right. In the next chapter, I will explain more about why I have chosen this as my definition; but I hope that even readers who quarrel with my selection of the term integrity to refer to the form of commitment that I describe will come away from the book understanding why the concept itself, whatever it may be called, is a vital one.

The word integrity comes from the same Latin root as *integer* and historically has been understood to carry much the same sense, the sense of wholeness. A person of integrity, like a whole number, is a whole person, a person somehow undivided. The word conveys not so much a single mindedness as a completeness; not the frenzy of a fanatic who wants to remake all the world in a single mold but the serenity of a person who is confident in the knowledge that he or she is living rightly. The person of integrity need not be a Gandhi but also cannot be a person who blows up buildings to make a point. A person of integrity lurks somewhere inside each of us: a person we feel we can trust to do right, to play by the rules, to keep commitments. Perhaps it is because we all sense the capacity for integrity within ourselves that we are able to notice and admire it even in people with whom, on many issues, we sharply disagree.

Indeed, one reason to focus on integrity as perhaps the first among the virtues that make for good character is that it is in some sense prior to everything else: the rest of what we think matters very little if we lack essential integrity, the courage of our convictions, the willingness to act and speak in behalf of what we know to be right. In an era when the American people are crying out for open discussion of morality—of right and wrong—the ideal of integrity seems a good place to begin. No matter what our politics, no matter what causes we may support, would anybody really want to be led or followed or assisted by people who lack integrity? People whose words we could not trust, whose motives we didn't respect, who might at any moment toss aside everything we thought we had in common and march off in some other direction?

The answer, of course, is no: we would not want leaders of that kind, even though we too often get them. The question is not only what integrity is and why it is valuable, but how we move our institutions, and our very lives closer to exemplifying it.

Integrity and Religion

The concept we are calling integrity has had little attention from philosophers, but has long been a central concern to the religions. Integrity, after all, is a kind of wholeness, and most religions teach that God calls us to an undivided life in accordance with divine command. In Islam, this notion is captured in the understanding that all rules, legal or moral, are guided by the sharia, the divine path that God directs humans to walk. In Judaism, study of the Torah and Talmud reveals the rules under which God's people are expected to live. And Christians are called by the Gospel to be "pure in heart" (Matt. 5:8), which implies an undividedness in following God's rules.

Indeed, although its antecedents may be traced to Aristotle, the basic concept of integrity was introduced to the Western tradition through the struggle of Christianity to find a guide for the well-lived life. The wholeness that the Christian tradition identified as central to life with integrity was a wholeness in obedience to God so that the well-lived life was a life that followed God's rules. Thomas Aquinas put it this way: "[T]he virtue of obedience is more praiseworthy than other moral virtues, seeing that by obedience a person gives up his own will for God's sake, and by other moral virtues something less." John Wesley, in a famous sermon, was more explicit: "[T]he nature of the covenant of grace gives you no ground, no encouragement at all, to set aside any instance or degree of obedience."

But obedience to what? Traditional religions teach that integrity is found in obedience to God. Moses Maimonides put the point most simply: "Everything that you do, do for the sake of God." And a professor W. S. Tyler, preaching a sermon at Amherst College in 1857, pointed the way to generalizing the concept beyond the religious sphere: "[I]ntegrity implies implicit obedience to the dictates of conscience; in other words, a heart and life habitually controlled by a sense of duty."

QUICK TIP

Make It A Personal Rule To Participate In Every Class

If you know you'll be called upon in class to make a comment or answer a question, you're likely to prepare better and be more attentive in class. So whether or not your professor calls on you, make it a personal rule to participate at least once in every class session. As you read or listen to a lecture, think of one honest question to raise or observation to offer. Don't sit back and let others dominate a class discussion; consider what is being said and respond to it. Knowing that you'll have to contribute in class will help you not only to take out-of-class preparation more seriously, but also to stay engaged and interested during class.

Re-Reading Questions

1. What evidence does Carter give to defend his hypothesis that America is having an integrity crisis? What examples does he use that might contradict this hypothesis?

2. Carter says that integrity requires three steps. What are they?

3. What is the connection, according to Carter, between integrity and "wholeness"? How does this relate to religion?

Discussion Questions

1. Is Carter right that, in America, "we care more about winning than about playing by the rules"? Can you think of some examples, either from your own personal experience or that of your family, friends, acquaintances, that support or refute Carter's assertion? In what ways is our culture supportive of integrity? In what ways is our culture ambivalent toward integrity?

2. What are some specific ways that integrity will be important in your college career academically, socially, personally? Based on your high school experience, do people usually demonstrate integrity in each of these situations? Why or why not? What do you perceive to be the rewards for acting with integrity at college? What are the potential consequences for not acting with integrity?

Discovery Questions

1. Review the "Code of Student Conduct" section of the Viking Code. List some of the explicitly stated behavioral expectations. How are these expectations related to integrity? What are some of the explicitly stated consequences for not acting with integrity? Be sure to discuss both academic and social expectations.

2. Set up an appointment with at least one, but preferably two or three, professors who have taught at Berry for ten years or more. Ask them for specific examples of times when students did not act with academic integrity—in other words, examples of cheating. What were the consequences? Did the professors believe these consequences were severe enough? Why or why not? Based on these conversations, how important is academic integrity to college professors? Do you see any difference between them and your high school teachers?

ACKNOWLEDGMENTS

Stephen Carter. "The Rules About the Rules" from *Integrity*. Copyright © 1996 by Stephen Carter. Reprinted by permission of Basic Books, a member of Perseus Books, L.L.C.

Robert Coles. "The Disparity Between Intellect and Character" from *The Chronicle of Higher Education*, 9/22/95. Reprinted by permission of the author.

Robert Hayden. "Those Winter Sundays" from Frederick Glaysher ed. *Collected Poems of Robert Hayden*. Copyright © 1962, 1978 by Liveright Publishing Corporation. Reprinted by permission of Liveright Publishing Corporation.

David Huddle. "The 'Banked Fires' of Robert Hayden's 'Those Winter Sundays'" from Robert Pack and Jay Parini, eds., *Touchstones: American Poets on a Favorite Poem*. Copyright © 1992 by the President and Fellows of Middlebury College. Reprinted by permission of the author.

Adrienne Rich. "Claiming an Education" from *On Lies, Secrets, and Silence: Selected Prose 1966–1978* by Adrienne Rich. Copyright © 1979 by W.W. Norton & Company, Inc. Reprinted by permission of the author and W.W. Norton & Company, Inc.

Beverly Daniel Tatum. "Overcoming the Culture of Silence About Race" from *The Chronicle of Higher Education*, 9/2/1997. Reprinted by permission of the author.

"To Alfred Corn: 30 May 62" from *The Habit of Being: Letters by Flannery O'Connor*, edited and selected by Sally Fitzgerald. Reprinted by permission of Farrar, Straus and Giroux, LLC.

Thanks to all of the writers who contributed to this book, and especially to Rebecca Phillips for help with manuscript preparation.